LOW-FAT COOKING
TO BEAT THE CLOCK

LOW-FAT COOKING

TO BEAT THE CLOCK

Delicious, Inspired Meals in 15 Minutes

by Sam Gugino   Photographs by Frankie Frankeny

CHRONICLE BOOKS

SAN FRANCISCO

Library of Congress Cataloging-in-Publication Data available.

ISBN 0-8118-2712-7

Printed in Hong Kong.

Prop Styling by Camella Haecker
Food Styling By Wesley Martin
Designed by Carpenter Design, San Francisco, CA.
Typesetting by Suzanne Scott
The photographer wishes to thank Bill LeBlond as always for his
streaming support, Jeremy Stout for his fabulous encouragement
and vision, Tim Carpenter for his collaboration with design and
photography, Cindy Blair, Wesley Martin, and Camella Haecker.

Distributed in Canada by Raincoast Books
9050 Shaughnessy Street
Vancouver, British Columbia V6P 6E5

10 9 8 7 6 5 4 3 2 1

Chronicle Books LLC
85 Second Street
San Francisco, California 94105

www.chroniclebooks.com

Acknowledgments

This book is dedicated to Art Milner, humor writer, frolicsome illustrator and painter, playwright, and a mentor to me in the early stages of my writing career. I first met Art in 1981 when I took his comedy writing class at Temple University in Philadelphia. Art encouraged me to pursue my writing and concentrate on the three things he felt I knew best: food, humor, and family. I always valued Art's counsel and took great delight in his mirth. Our friendship was cut short by Art's untimely death in 1989. But his drawings, which hang in my apartment, are a constant reminder of his influence in my life.

I owe an enormous debt to my recipe testers. After I tested the recipes, I gave them to these volunteers to try out in their home kitchens. I wanted to find out if the recipes could be done in fifteen minutes, or close to it, and if the dishes were enjoyable. The feedback from the testers was invaluable. Far from being a rubber stamp for the author, the testers frequently gave me a good going over. They questioned methods, suggested new ingredients, and ultimately passed judgment on each dish. While I didn't always agree with them, I made many changes based on their comments. So hats off to:

Marilyn Acker, Diane Ayala, Patty Beeken, Jill Rovitzky Black, Maryann Bolles, Thelma R. Booth, Donna L. Borden, Dixie Bosley, Kelly Bosley, Jeanne Brophy, Dave Brown, Tamie Callahan, Susan Cardenez, Larry Challacombe, Pamela Clausen, Mimi Connelly, Maria Dean Curran, Tom and Bonnie Davies, Cheryl B. Dawson, Nancy Deboy, Corinne Derry, Maria L. Detrick, Karen J. Duhart, Barbara L. Dundon, Lou Anne Dunfee, Terri Ebaugh, KT Ellenbecker, Dee Evans, Sherry Finnamore, Lois K. Fletcher, Annie Foerster, Debby Fortune, Jane Frantz, Tanya L. Girman, Mary W. Goad, Eugenia E. Gratto, Shannon Green, Joan Gregory, C. R. Griffin, Jr., DDS, Jane Hibbard, Jennifer J. Hill, Sandy (Sam) Hill, Lucinda Jenkins, Bob and Caroline Kearney, Kendra Knight, Allyson Langston, Kathy Ledesma, Glenda Liebsack, Linda Brecht Marr, L. Gilman Martin, Judith Martir, Alice Masters, Pat Mater, Jennifer Mayne, Heather McGill and John Sedore, Jerry McPhee, Melissa Mersits, Jeanne Miller, Ellen Monrad, Angela Montez, Janet Morrissey, Monique Nash, Yasmin Nissen, James A. Nugent Jr., Sandy Olson, Joyce Osborn, Kathleen Lowe Owen, Terri Parsons, Lisa Payne and Mike Chirico, Suzanne Pickett, Arryn Pidwell and Marcus Breaden, Peter Rasmussen, Ruth Roberts, Teresa Rockefeller, Lois M. Rosenblum, Judie Ross-Bales, Ann P. Rowell, Stu Rubin, Vida Russell, Marion Russo-Lleras, Jennifer Salerno, Eileen Scheffel, Dona Scott, Beth Seebach, Gloria Self, Kimberly Madejczyk Shelton, Tom Sherman, Karen Sidebotham, Pat Sinclair, Rebecca Staffel, Andy and Amy Stahl, David C. Stokes, Elizabeth A. Stout, Sandy Szwarc, Tami Thiesenhusen, Raye Ann Tiedemann, Richard H. Wagner, Joan A. Waldron, Mimi and Bud Weiss, Ed Wheeless, Rachel Wilson, Mary Ann Wisman, Pauline S. Yoder, and Carolyn Zamorano.

I'd also like to thank the staff of Chronicle books, including Bill LeBlond, and especially senior publicist Michele Fuller, an author's dream come true; my agent Jane Dystel; Andy Schloss; Harold McGee; Lisa Callaghan; James Symons; Lynn Hill; and finally, last but not least, my best friend, closest advisor, Web mistress, recipe testing coordinator, newsletter editor, and wife of twenty-five years, Mary Lee Keane.

Table of Contents

Introduction

In *Cooking to Beat the Clock: Delicious, Inspired Meals in 15 Minutes,* I wrote about how to put great food on the table in less time than it takes most pizzas to be delivered. But were you satisfied? Nooooooooo.

That's because like most Americans you're not only hungry for good food and in a hurry, you're also watching your waistline most of the time. But is it possible to prepare a dinner in fifteen minutes that's delicious *and* low in fat? You bet it is. Here's how.

Like *Cooking to Beat the Clock,* this book is built on the four pillars of Flavor, Organization, Focus, and Creativity. Flavor means a pantry well stocked with ingredients that have great taste and texture. Organization is having the right equipment in the right place to simplify and speed up preparation. Focus requires being single minded about getting the meal out in a hurry. Creativity involves thinking beyond recipes so you don't always have to follow a specific formula. This book also keeps an eye on using less fat. Thus, pantry suggestions listed under Flavor in the following chapter have a slimmer look with items such as nonfat yogurt.

The sixty recipes in this book, like those in *Cooking to Beat the Clock,* are designed as meals, not just dishes. Portions are intended for humans, not hummingbirds, unlike many low-fat recipes in other cookbooks. As I write this, I am reading a recipe for turkey cacciatore from a low-fat cookbook. It serves four people and calls for eight ounces of turkey. My Chicken Cacciatore (page 48), which takes half the time—and includes polenta!—has twice the amount of poultry. Another cookbook, which claims its recipes are 99 percent fat-free, calls for an ounce—an ounce!—of pork per person in a stew. Then it says "serve a generous ¾ cup

to each person." There's nothing generous about a ¾-cup serving unless we're talking about a snack. My Pork and Sweet Potato Stew with Couscous (page 31) contains five ounces of pork per serving plus a healthy amount of sweet potatoes and couscous.

While some low-fat recipes reduce portion sizes to microscopic levels, others lower the fat so drastically that the resulting dishes are often bland and boring. There's no getting around the fact that a certain amount of fat is necessary for what food industry folks call "mouthfeel," that sensation on the palate that tells your brain whether what you've just tasted is worth finishing, or not. I've always felt it doesn't matter how low in fat a dish is if people don't eat it.

So isn't it better to eat a Taco Salad (page 130), which has 10.62 grams of fat per serving and 28.73 percent fat, but which volunteer recipe tester Jane Hibbard described as "wonderful . . . we all thought the dressing was superb," than a dish with 15 percent fat, which leaves you unsatisfied? Of course, sometimes, you get great taste *and* extremely low fat, as with Monkfish Osso Buco (page 73). Tester Marion Russo-Lleras found it "absolutely rich and delicious" and "very satisfying" despite only 7.10 grams of fat per serving and an overall fat content of 12.92 percent. (All the recipes in this book have been analyzed by the respected Hill Nutrition Associates, Inc., and list calories, the amount of fat and saturated fat, and the percentage of fat.)

Nutritionists tell us that the ideal diet is one in which the percentage of overall calories from fat is less than 30 percent. My aim in this book was to create recipes with fat calories that are less than 30 percent or which contain less than 12 grams of fat per serving, or both. The reason I include grams of fat in addition to the percentage of fat is that sometimes percentages can be misleading. For example, my Cobb Salad (page 123) has only 8.8 grams of fat per serving. But because it has a mere 248.10 calories, the percentage of fat is 31.28 percent. From my perspective, the percentage of fat in each serving of this dish is far less significant than the total grams of fat and overall calories.

Nonetheless, you may want to stay closer to, say, 20 percent fat. (In fact, half of the recipes in the book are below 20 percent fat. One-fifth are below 15 percent.) One way to achieve a lower percentage of fat is to cut back on the four to six ounces of meat, seafood, or poultry that almost all recipes have. For example, use four ounces of pork tenderloin per serving in the Pork and Sweet Potato Stew with Couscous (page 31) instead of five ounces. Or reduce portion sizes by serving one extra person. While all recipes in this book serve four people, my volunteer recipe testers frequently told me some of the dishes they cooked could serve five or six people.

In addition to the amount of fat we consume, the type of fat is also important. Our diets should contain less saturated fats (like butter), which come primarily from animal sources (though coconut oil has more saturated fat than butter), less hydrogenated oils (vegetable oils treated to become solid at room temperature, like margarine), and more mono-unsaturated fats (like olive and canola oil), which some studies suggest help lower blood cholesterol. This book relies primarily on olive oil and canola oil, which are among the top oils in percentage of monounsaturated fats.

That said, you may be surprised to see a tablespoon or two of butter or heavy cream here and there. The reason is that mouthfeel I mentioned earlier. Years ago I learned that a judicious amount of fat, even saturated fat, can add an amazing degree of richness to a dish, especially if it is added just before serving. Thus, for example, I've added two table-spoons of heavy cream to the Spaghetti Squash with Turkey Bolognese Sauce on page 53. Yet despite this seeming extravagance, each serving contains only 9 grams of fat, and the overall percentage of fat in the dish is 24.75.

I also believe that to compensate for the reduced fat, you've got to satisfy the senses in other ways. Unfortunately, time constraints don't allow for flavors to develop during long, slow roasting, braising, or caramelizing. So I've intensified flavors by using more herbs and spices.

As with my previous book, I use fresh ingredients whenever possible, though I do use canned and frozen items when the quality is good. I've used the same logic when it comes to low-fat ingredients. For example, oil sprays can reduce the amount of cooking fat significantly without affecting the quality of the final dish. Part-skim ricotta is a very acceptable substitute for whole-milk ricotta.

While you can expect some surprising, even dramatic satisfaction from the recipes you cook from this book, don't expect those love handles to melt off the moment you finish your first dish. For that you need a comprehensive program that includes, among other things, regular exercise. But it can be done. Several years ago, while at the *San Jose Mercury News,* I wrote a series of articles called "Fat City" chronicling my 30-day low-fat diet in which I lost 10 pounds, 2 inches from my waist, and 62 points on my cholesterol—all without feeling as if I was starving myself. To create this book I've taken what I learned from that series, combined it with additional low-fat cooking experience in the ensuing years, and fused it all with my quick-cooking expertise. The result, I believe, is something you can use to eat happily as well as healthfully for many years to come.

If you have comments or questions about the recipes or information in this book, or about quick cooking in general, I'd like to hear from you. Please feel free to e-mail me at: sam@samcooks.com, or visit my Web site, www.samcooks.com, where you can sign up for my free newsletter.

Flavor, Organization, Focus, and Creativity

FLAVOR

Flavor means a pantry—which also includes the refrigerator and freezer—well stocked with flavorful ingredients. The last thing you want to do when you're hungry and in a hurry is to run out to the store. Having ingredients that pack lots of taste is important because you don't have much time for flavors to develop, the way you would in long-simmering stews, for example.

Flavorful ingredients are even more important for low-fat meals in fifteen minutes. Fats provide a great deal of the sensory satisfaction we get from food. If we reduce the amount of fat in our diet, we need to compensate with other ingredients that provide an alternative to the "mouthfeel" that fats give us. And when we do use fat-laden ingredients they must be sufficiently flavorful so we can use less of them.

For example, in Fettuccine with Pesto, Potatoes, and Tomatoes (page 82), I use one tablespoon of olive oil for my pesto sauce instead of the normal 1/3 to 1/2 cup. But that olive oil is absolutely the most flavorful oil I can afford. And isn't it better to spend money on good food than on cockamamie diet plans?

Fresh herbs and spices also add flavor. The most vital seasoning, however, is salt. In many instances when my recipe testers said a dish was a bit bland, it was inadequately salted. With the exception of specific amounts of salt for cooking pasta, rice, and some vegetables, recipes tell readers to "season to taste" with salt because everyone's tolerance for salt is different. But unless you're on a sodium-restricted diet, don't stint on the salt. Salting at the table isn't always a good solution because the salt doesn't get fully integrated into the dish.

As with *Cooking to Beat the Clock,* I use fresh ingredients in this book whenever possible. Canned or frozen ingredients are used judiciously, including those that are reduced in fat or fat-free, such as reduced-fat coconut milk for dishes like Curried Shrimp and Corn Chowder (page 103) and fat-free canned chicken stock, which I use constantly.

Low-fat and especially nonfat ingredients should be purchased with care. For example, with a few exceptions, such as nonfat yogurt, my general rule of thumb with dairy products is to avoid any in which the fat is cut by more than 50 percent because the loss of flavor and texture isn't worth the reduction in fat.

Use the following pantry suggestions as a guide. Tailor your pantry to the way you eat, whether that means more Asian or vegetarian ingredients or just foods that you like. However your pantry is stocked, read labels for fat content. For foods without nutritional labeling such as meats, poultry, and seafood, get a reliable book that lists fat content and other nutritional values. (For this book I used *The Nutribase Nutrition Facts Desk Reference* by Dr. Art Ulene.) Depending on your family size and storage space, shop once a month for dry storage or freezer items, two or three times a month for refrigerated items like Parmesan cheese and eggs, and twice a week for most perishable foods.

ARTICHOKE HEARTS: Packed in water, usually in 15-ounce cans, not oil-packed artichokes in smaller jars. For salads and pastas.

CURED MEATS AND SAUSAGES:

PROSCIUTTO: Because Prosciutto di Parma, the authentic ham from Italy, as well as other hams such as San Daniele and Carpegna, are so intensely flavored, a little goes a long way. For cold preparations, use within a few days. For cooked dishes, refrigerate up to ten days.

BACON: Regular bacon must be used sparingly, cooked crisp, and drained well as in Cobb Salad (page 123). Canadian bacon, used in Seafood Cassoulet (page 75), contains about one-third the fat of regular bacon and roughly the same as turkey bacon used in Spaghetti Squash with Turkey Bolognese Sauce (page 53).

SAUSAGES: Poultry, game, and seafood sausages offer low-fat alternatives to the normally fatty pork sausages. (Don't assume that poultry automatically means low fat, however. Fatty ingredients like skin may be mixed in.) I keep Hillshire Farm's turkey kielbasa (used in Paella, page 101, and Black Bean Soup with Turkey Kielbasa, page 108) in the freezer because it contains only 2.5 grams of fat per ounce, and it doesn't taste like Naugahyde, the way some low-fat and fat-free sausages do.

HAMS: There are many lean domestic hams now on the market. Smoked ham generally has more flavor and thus can be used in smaller amounts. (See Black-Eyed Pea Soup with Collard Greens, page 111.)

BEANS, CANNED: An excellent source of low-fat protein. Quality can vary among brands. Chickpeas (garbanzos), cannellini beans, and black beans make up my pantry's canned bean triumvirate. Others to consider are red kidney, pink, pinto, navy, Great Northern, and white beans. Canned black-eyed peas are used in Black-Eyed Pea Soup with Collard Greens (page 111).

BREADS: Pita bread, used in the Greek Bread Salad with Feta Cheese (page 126), is often made without fat and freezes well. I don't like corn tortillas unless they're freshly made. Flour tortillas usually have too much fat, so I prefer low-fat flour tortillas for the Turkey Tacos with Red Pepper Salsa (page 49) and Burritos with Braised Vegetables and Pumpkin Seeds (page 142). They will last a week or more in the refrigerator and can be frozen. (Before freezing, separate the tortillas with wax paper to prevent them from sticking together.)

BUTTER: Judicious amounts can add a sweet and creamy flavor to dishes and can help replace the mouthfeel lost by reducing overall fat in a recipe. I use unsalted butter because I think it tastes better than salted butter. But it is more perishable, so I keep one stick in the refrigerator and the rest in the freezer. Frozen butter defrosts quickly in a microwave oven.

CAPERS: These flower buds pack lots of flavor with no fat. They are most commonly available in brine and come in two sizes. The smaller nonpareil capers from France are of better quality and more convenient because they don't need to be chopped.

CHEESE:

Generally, it's better to use less regular cheese than more reduced-fat cheese. For example, only two ounces of blue cheese works fine in the Cobb Salad (page 123). I use Danish blue, Bleu d'Auvergne, or a good quality domestic blue.

CREAM CHEESES: Low-fat versions, particularly those flavored with herbs, garlic, and other seasonings, can make quick pasta sauces. Simply toss them with hot pasta and some of the pasta cooking water.

FETA: There are many styles of this crumbly chalk-white cheese, used in Greek Bread Salad with Feta Cheese (page 126) and Pasta with Broccoli Raab and Feta Cheese (page 85). Sheep's milk feta usually has less fat than cow's milk feta but isn't as widely available. Store in a plastic container in the refrigerator up to a week.

GOAT CHEESES: There are a wide range of domestic and imported cheeses, fresh and aged. Not all goat cheese is lower in fat. Only fresh, soft goat cheese is about 6 grams of fat per ounce, versus 8.5 grams per ounce for semisoft and 10.1 grams for hard. The trade-off is that hard goat cheese is more intensely flavored because it has less moisture. Coach Farms, one of my favorite brands, has a reduced-fat soft cheese. Fresh goat cheese will keep only a few days under refrigeration unless vacuum sealed. Aged goat cheese lasts several days.

PARMESAN: Parmigiano-Reggiano, the real thing, is worth the extra cost. Already relatively low in fat at 7 grams an ounce, Parmigiano-Reggiano's incomparable flavor can be spread further by grating. If possible, grate as needed, instead of using already grated cheese. If you prefer the convenience of grated Parmigiano-Reggiano, buy it from a place that sells a lot of it and store in the freezer up to two months. A piece of ungrated Parmigiano-Reggiano should be used up within a few weeks.

PECORINO ROMANO: A sheep's milk grating cheese with more bite than Parmesan for more rustic presentations. Store it like Parmesan.

RICOTTA: Part-skim-milk ricotta is a good, low-fat substitute for soft goat cheese in pasta dishes such as the Pasta Primavera (page 91).

OTHERS: Cabot's reduced fat Cheddar (50 percent less fat, not 75 percent) is one of the better lower-fat cheeses, as is Swiss-type Lite Jarlsberg.

DAIRY, OTHER: You don't lose that much when you step down from whole milk to nonfat yogurt. However, some brands of nonfat sour cream can be chalky. Low-fat cottage cheese could be used as a substitute for ricotta.

EGGS: At five grams of fat each, eggs are not out of the question on a low-fat diet, which is why I have included Salmon Galette with Eggs (page 64). Store eggs in their containers in the refrigerator. The door is not cold enough. Fat-free egg substitutes can be used in dishes like Spaghetti Carbonara with Prosciutto and Peas (page 86).

FRUITS, DRIED: Concentrated flavor and very little fat make them good ingredients for low-fat meals. They are particularly suited for North African–inspired dishes like Pork and Sweet Potato Stew with Couscous (page 31), which uses dried apricots, and the Indian-influenced Vegetable Biryani (page 135), which uses raisins. Dates and figs are good candidates, but not the hard Turkish figs, which take too long to soften.

FRUITS, FRESH: SEE PRODUCE

GRAINS:

COUSCOUS: Actually a kind of pasta, though used like a grain. Almost always found in instant form and the quality is often good.

POLENTA: This cornmeal mush takes too long to cook on the stove, though in a microwave oven it's faster. I use instant polenta, which takes only a few minutes on the stove.

RICE: I use fragrant basmati rice exclusively in this book because this slender, long-grain rice cooks quicker than normal long-grain rice. Indian basmati is available in many supermarkets as well as by mail order (page 149). Basmati is also produced in the United States as Texmati.

HERBS:

DRIED: Sage leaves (not ground), thyme, rosemary, mint, and marjoram are decent substitutes for fresh herbs. Oregano is actually better dried, but only the sweeter, more fragrant Mediterranean oregano, usually labeled Greek, Turkish, or Sicilian. Ideally purchase it in bunches in Middle Eastern markets or better food stores. Bay leaves are almost always sold dried. Herbes de Provence, the herb blend, is a terrific all-purpose seasoning. When well-sealed and stored away from heat, dried herbs keep six to twelve months.

FRESH: Most supermarkets carry several fresh herbs. I use mint, basil, thyme, chives, tarragon, rosemary, dill, and cilantro most often. For parsley, I prefer the more flavorful flat-leaf, or Italian type. Fresh herbs will last up to one week, loosely bagged in plastic and stored in the crisper section of the refrigerator.

LEMONS AND LIMES: Available year-round, so there's no excuse for buying the bottled stuff, which doesn't give you the flavorful zests either. Well-sealed in plastic bags, they keep up to six weeks in the refrigerator.

MAYONNAISE AND SALAD DRESSINGS: I use Hellmann's (or Best Foods) Light Mayonnaise, which contains about half the fat and calories of regular mayonnaise. Nonfat mayonnaise is dreadful.

MEAT AND POULTRY, FROZEN: Lean cuts of beef, whole pork tenderloins, veal cutlets, boneless chicken breasts, and turkey cutlets are good to have in the freezer. Wrap them in individual or one-meal portions for easier defrosting. (See Meat and Poultry chapters.)

MILK, CANNED: Evaporated skim milk makes a decent substitute for cream in dishes like Quick Blanquette de Veau (page 29). Light coconut milk, in Curried Shrimp and Corn Chowder (page 103), is an excellent stand-in for the full-fat version.

MILK, REFRIGERATED: I use 1-percent and 2-percent milk, depending on the situation. Buttermilk, despite its name, is almost always low in fat and gives a creamy, tangy taste to dressings and cold soups.

MUSHROOMS: Most markets now carry several kinds of mushrooms. An increasing number of stores also carry sliced mushrooms for convenience.

MUSTARDS: It wasn't until I wrote about mustards for my "Tastes" column in the *Wine Spectator* that I realized there are literally thousands of them in various categories, all with little or no fat. Dijon is a must. Also consider flavored Dijons (such as tarragon, used in Chicken à la Moutarde, page 46); sweet and hot mustards like the one used in Honey-Mustard Salmon with Cucumber-Dill Salad (page 63); coarse grain; herb; hot pepper; and horseradish mustards.

NUTS AND SEEDS: While low in saturated fat, nuts are fat-dense. So use them sparingly. To maximize flavor, toast them as in the Moroccan Lemon Chicken (page 40). Sesame seeds, used in Pork and Sweet Potato Stew with Couscous (page 31), are great because they stretch easily. Nuts go rancid quite quickly, so buy them already sealed (not from open bulk containers) and store them in the freezer, where they'll last up to six months.

OILS AND OIL SPRAYS:

NUT AND SEED OILS: Walnut is the most common nut oil, but others like almond, hazelnut, and pecan are becoming more available. Oils made from toasted nuts or seeds, like Asian sesame oil, have more intense flavor. Use these oils as you use high-quality extra-virgin olive oils, in cold dishes or drizzled on hot foods just before serving, as in the Asian Chicken Noodle Soup (page 113).

OLIVE OIL: Go for the most flavorful extra-virgin oil you can afford, because you'll be doling it out by the teaspoon, not by the cup. "Extra light" or "light" oils don't have less fat—all olive oils have about 14 grams of fat per tablespoon—just a lighter olive oil flavor.

OTHER OILS: I use canola oil as my neutral cooking oil for its heart-healthy qualities and relatively high smoke point. Flavored oils, such as those with basil and roasted garlic, are time-savers because they eliminate at least one ingredient. Well-sealed in a cool, dry place (not the refrigerator), oils will last several months.

OIL SPRAYS: A spritz on a nonstick skillet allows you to sauté meats and vegetables with almost no fat. I use canola and olive oil sprays most often. There are also butter-flavor sprays and flavored olive oil sprays. (See Low-Fat and Quick-Cooking Tips, page 23.)

OLIVES: Because they are loaded with fat, use them like nuts. Stick with brine-cured rather than oil-cured olives. Pitted olives save time. Jars of green pitted cocktail olives—plain or pimiento stuffed—keep in the refrigerator for several weeks or more.

ONION FAMILY:

ONIONS: White, Spanish, or yellow onions (known collectively as storage onions) can be used in any recipe that calls for cooked onions. A small onion is about four ounces, medium about eight ounces, and large about twelve ounces. For raw onions, use Vidalia or similar sweet onions. Because they run a bit bigger than storage onions, I list them by weight (i.e., "four ounces sweet onion such as Vidalia"). Red onions are usually between storage and sweet onions in pungency. I keep storage onions in the refrigerator, where they last several weeks. Sweet and red onions should be kept cool but not refrigerated and consumed within a few weeks.

OTHER: Garlic will last several weeks without refrigeration if kept cool. When a clove is called for, it should be good sized. Chopped or whole peeled garlic in jars is an acceptable convenience but garlic powder is not. Shallots will last several weeks without refrigeration if kept cool. A head or bulb of shallots will often contain more than one clove. When a shallot is called for, it means a single clove. Green onions (or scallions) will last up to five days under refrigeration. The green tops can be substituted for chives.

PASTA: Except for the *acini di pepe* (or pastina) used in my Broccoli and Pasta Soup (page 102) and medium egg noodles in the Beef Stroganoff (page 27), I use capellini (also known as angel hair or *capelli d'angelo*) exclusively as my dried pasta because it cooks the fastest. I prefer Italian pasta because it is firmer. Fresh pasta, regardless of the shape, cooks as fast as or faster than dried capellini.

More and more supermarkets carry a variety of fresh pasta. While dried pasta, as the saying goes, lasts longer than many marriages, fresh pasta lasts one to two weeks under refrigeration. Rice noodles, used in Asian Chicken Noodle Soup (page 113), and other Asian noodles can be seen more frequently in mainstream markets.

PASTES: While extremely convenient, most pastes, such as commercial pesto or tapenade, are fat landmines. Read the labels.

PRODUCE: Though a cliché, it's true that one should pick seasonal produce at the peak of ripeness. So forget tomatoes in January, even if they look pretty. When produce is in season, shop frequently for perishable items like salad greens, cooking greens, green beans, asparagus, broccoli, zucchini, and corn, all of which will last up to three days, though corn tastes best if consumed immediately. Other produce, such as celery, can last a week or more under refrigeration if sealed in plastic bags; carrots and potatoes last up to five weeks. If kept cool, but not refrigerated, sweet potatoes will keep up to four weeks.

Take advantage of the myriad of convenience items such as shredded cabbage for coleslaw, broccoli florets for stir-fries, cleaned spinach, and salad mixes, as well as chopped vegetables from your supermarket's salad bar, if it has one. Cooked potatoes can be found in refrigerated produce cases. Yes, these items cost more per pound. But you won't use that much. And you are saving time. On her second try at Tortilla Soup (page 110), tester Kimberly Madejczyk Shelton used trimmed and cut celery and minced garlic from a jar, which helped her cut preparation time by more than a third.

14

ROASTED RED BELL PEPPERS: Seeded, peeled, and packed in jars, they can be used in many dishes, from Paella (page 101) to Turkey Tacos with Red Pepper Salsa (page 49). And they have almost no fat. This category includes pimientos, the mild, heart-shaped sweet red pepper, which is sometimes available chopped.

SALSAS AND CHUTNEYS: Both offer intense and multiple flavors that can enhance a sauce or dressing with very little or no fat. Or they can be served on their own to dress up plain grilled meat, chicken, or fish.

SALT: I've become a big fan of sea salt since my last book. It's milder than other salts, even kosher salt, my second choice. However, because it is pricey and less noticeable in cooked dishes, I generally reserve sea salt for uncooked dishes.

SAUCES: If you use soy sauce frequently, consider having two kinds on hand: dark soy for heartier dishes and a lighter soy sauce for light dishes and dressings. Fish sauces are great flavor boosters and don't taste as strongly as they smell. A little hoisin or black bean sauce can add a jolt to Asian dishes like Clams and Asparagus with Black Bean Sauce (page 66). For non-Asian dishes, try Worcestershire sauce. Sometimes all a dish needs is a splash of hot pepper sauce. Tabasco is the most common, but habanero sauce, despite its searing heat, has lots of flavor.

SEAFOOD, CANNED:

ANCHOVIES: Just a fillet or two adds enormous flavor to many dishes like Pasta with Tuna Sauce (page 96), without much fat but with heart-healthy Omega 3 fatty acids. Don't use fillets wrapped around capers. Anchovy paste in tubes lasts almost forever in the refrigerator, but doesn't give you the flavor of high-quality anchovy fillets from Spain or Sicily.

CLAMS: After tuna, the most versatile canned seafood for chowders and pastas. I prefer chopped to minced.

TUNA: Fancy albacore packed in water has considerably less fat than tuna packed in oil. Quality varies widely among brands.

OTHER: The salmon used in the Salmon Galette with Eggs (page 64) is pink boneless and skinless salmon, which is less fatty than sockeye salmon and more convenient because there are no bones or skin. Canned sardines and mussels are not used in this book but are candidates for the pantry. For example, mussels could be used in quick pasta dishes (like canned clams).

SEAFOOD, CURED: Smoked or cured seafood, particularly salmon, is great for quick meals because it is already cooked and you don't need much, as in the Warm Potato Salad with Smoked Salmon and Cabbage (page 117). It will keep about a week under refrigeration and can be frozen for up to three months.

SEAFOOD, FRESH: See the Seafood chapter.

SEAFOOD, FROZEN: Use frozen crab and shrimp, not canned. The crab could be used in Crab and Oyster Gumbo (page 104) and the shrimp in Curried Shrimp and Corn Chowder (page 103). Some companies like Turner New Zealand (see Mail-Order Sources, page 149) offer frozen cleaned and cooked clams and mussels in the shell.

SPICES: I grind small batches of whole spices like cumin, allspice, and dried ginger root in a minichopper (see Organization, page 18) for more flavor. As needed, grind black peppercorns in a pepper mill and nutmeg with a nutmeg grater. Other important spices include red pepper flakes, cayenne pepper, saffron threads (not ground), curry powder, candied (also called crystallized) ginger, and paprika (both hot and sweet). Less often I use Chinese five-spice powder, caraway seeds, juniper berries, fennel seeds, chili powder, and other dried chiles such as ancho, New Mexico, and chipotle peppers. (Chipotles also come canned in a savory adobo sauce.) Ground spices last up to eighteen months, whole spices up to two years. Store them away from heat and light.

Pickled sliced jalapeño peppers are a very good substitute for fresh jalapeños and last for months in the refrigerator. Fresh ginger is an important part of my spice collection. Once cut, wrap it in a paper towel and put it in a plastic bag in the refrigerator where it will last a few weeks or more. Chopped ginger in a jar, much like chopped garlic, can also be found in some markets.

STOCK (BROTH): Chicken stock is the most versatile canned stock. I like Health Valley fat-free, reduced sodium chicken stock. Though salty, bottled clam juice is very handy as a seafood or fish stock alternative in dishes like Cacciucco (page 76). Canned beef stock can also be quite salty. Canned vegetable stocks are more evident than they were a few years ago. Some gourmet markets offer refrigerated "homemade" stocks, which can be frozen. Pastes or bases, mixed with water to form stocks, are usually preferable to bouillon cubes.

THICKENERS: I generally use cornstarch, but arrowroot is fine, though more expensive. Both work more efficiently than flour.

TOMATOES, CANNED: Canned tomatoes are among the most important pantry items for low-fat cooking, especially for pasta dishes like Capellini with Southwestern-style Clam Sauce (page 81) and Spaghetti all'Amatriciana (page 93). Canned tomatoes are particularly convenient if crushed or diced. Stewed tomatoes are chunky seasoned tomatoes that can have ethnic twists such as Mexican or Italian-style. Smooth and seasoned tomato sauce is especially useful for dishes like Spaghetti Squash with Turkey Bolognese Sauce (page 53). Because tomato paste is generally used in small amounts, buy it in tubes, like anchovy paste, and store it similarly.

TOMATOES, SUN-DRIED: Easily reconstituted with boiling water and considerably less fatty (and cheaper) than those marinated in oil in jars. Sun-dried tomato bits can be sprinkled into rice, pasta, vegetable dishes, and salad dressings.

VEGETABLES, CANNED OR BOTTLED: In addition to those mentioned earlier (such as artichoke hearts and roasted peppers), consider canned beets for Beef and Beet Salad with Horseradish Cream Dressing (page 128) or for a quick cold soup. Canned corn can be used in soups like Curried Shrimp and Corn Chowder (page 103). Sliced water chestnuts are good for soups such as Asian Chicken Noodle Soup (page 113), salads, and stir-fries like Spicy Chicken and Broccoli Stir-Fry (page 43). Canned mild chiles are handy for Mexican and Southwestern dishes like Tortilla Soup (page 110). Pickles, whether sweet or sour, can perk up dressings and composed salads like Beef and Beet Salad with Horseradish Cream Dressing (page 128).

VEGETABLES, FRESH: See Produce.

VEGETABLES, FROZEN: Peas, as used in the Spaghetti Carbonara with Prosciutto and Peas (page 86), corn, broccoli florets, and lima beans (used in the Vegetable Biryani, page 135) are the frozen vegetables I use most often. Frozen leaf spinach and corn are also good. Frozen hash-brown potatoes are used in Steak Diana with Skinny Jack Potatoes (page 28).

VINEGAR: A great source of nonfat flavor in cold dishes and a good substitute for alcohol when deglazing skillets for quick sauces in sautéed dishes. I use balsamic, sherry, and red wine vinegars most often. Balsamics come in many quality levels; the better ones are good enough to use as sauces or dressings by themselves. Raspberry is the most common of the many delicious fruit vinegars. Consorzio makes wonderful passion fruit and mango vinegars. Most fruit vinegars are less acidic than wine vinegars. For less acid without fruit flavor, use cider or rice wine vinegar.

WINES, LIQUEURS, AND SPIRITS: Never cook with any alcoholic beverage you wouldn't drink. Instead of opening a bottle of white wine for just a half cup, try dry vermouth. It's fortified to a higher proof, so you can use half the amount, and it lasts two months or more in the refrigerator. Dry sherry has the same durability. A good brandy has many uses and can often be substituted for other spirits.

TOP TWELVE FAT FIGHTERS

These ingredients have little or no fat and should be in everyone's pantry.

* Vinegars—from balsamic to mango

* Lemons and limes—peels and juice

* Tomatoes—fresh, canned, or dried

* Capers—small nonpareil, if possible

* Beans—from black to pinto

* Onion Family—garlic, onions, scallions, and shallots

* Fresh Herbs—especially basil, flat-leaf parsley, thyme, tarragon, rosemary, chives, dill, and cilantro

* Spices—especially black pepper, sea salt, cumin, ginger, curry powder, nutmeg, hot pepper (like cayenne or red pepper flakes), saffron, and paprika

* Mustards—from Dijon to honey mustard

* Roasted Red Bell Peppers—or pimientos

* Wine and Spirits—especially dry vermouth, sherry, and brandy

* Fat-free stocks and broths

ORGANIZATION

Organization means having the right equipment for fast meal preparation and having it easily accessible. A 12-inch, nonstick skillet is ideal for sautéing meat, fish, and poultry for four people without using much oil. The width also allows vegetables to boil quickly and liquids for sauces to reduce rapidly because there is more surface area over the heat.

Though we usually sauté in a skillet, a sauté pan is different from a skillet. A 12-inch, nonstick sauté pan does all a skillet does, but its straight sides (as opposed to the sloping sides of a skillet) give it more capacity (four quarts or more) that enables you to make quick soups and stews. Both the skillet and sauté pan should have covers, which increase pressure and thus the speed at which food cooks. Both should also be made of a heavy-gauge metal (with an aluminum or copper core) to conduct heat evenly. Store these pans carefully—put paper towels on the surface of the pans if they're going to be stacked—and use nonstick utensils to avoid scratching.

I like 10-inch (or larger), cast-iron skillets for high-heat cooking where a nonstick surface isn't crucial, as in Tuna Steak au Poivre with Buttermilk Mashed Potatoes (page 60). Well-seasoned, cast-iron skillets don't need much cooking fat, and they last forever. Cast-iron pans also come with ridges (and nonstick surfaces) to simulate grilling. Dutch ovens are often made of enameled cast iron and can be used in lieu of sauté pans for soups, stews, and quickly braised vegetables, like the napa cabbage in Pan-Seared Scallops with Napa Cabbage and Gingered Carrots (page 70).

Though primarily for sautéing, braising, steaming, and stir-frying, a wok can also be used as a mixing bowl. While classic woks are made of rolled steel, which should be treated like cast-iron skillets, they also come with nonstick surfaces.

Invert the ring that comes with the wok so it sits closer to the flame for more intense heat. Electric burners on high provide more heat than gas ranges.

I use a 2-quart saucepan for rice and a larger, heavier saucepan for polenta. Larger, thinner-gauge saucepans are good for boiling potatoes quickly because they have a wider surface area. For smaller jobs, like warming milk for mashed potatoes, I use a 1-quart saucepan. An 8-quart-capacity pasta pot is essential, not just for pasta but for boiling and steaming. A pasta pot with a colander insert allows you to easily dump drained pasta next door into a wok or sauté pan. However, a separate, 12-inch colander works just as well.

Most folks think a food processor is about as necessary in the kitchen as an espresso machine. But when volunteer Tami Thiesenhusen used hers to test Vegetable Biryani (page 135), she said: "I haven't used my food processor in a while and dragging it out for this recipe made me remember how easy it makes chopping and how much I love using it." I use the stainless steel cutting or chopping blade 90 percent of the time for purees, salsas, dressings, and chopping. Assume this blade is to be used unless the shredding or slicing discs are specified.

I also have a minichopper, which is about the size of a coffee grinder and costs only a few dollars more. The reversible blade chops nuts, seeds, and spices on one side and ingredients like garlic on the other. However, when making a dressing with garlic or fresh ginger, I use the full-size food processor.

Many people use the microwave oven only for defrosting or reheating. But it does a good job of cooking vegetables, rice, and potatoes. (It also makes easy polenta, though not as fast as instant on the stove.) The microwave also frees up more room on the stove. Still, I don't use it extensively, and I normally give conventional cooking methods as alternatives when I do.

You can cook quite well with only three knives: a chef's knife 8 inches or more in length, a paring knife, and perhaps a serrated knife for tomatoes and bread. Any knife should be sharp. I use a Chef's Choice sharpening machine because a sharpening steel isn't enough. Kitchen scissors can be used for a variety of tasks, from cutting sun-dried tomatoes into strips and snipping herbs like chives to trimming fat from chicken breasts.

Since not everyone has a butcher to pound chicken breasts into cutlets for faster cooking, you'll probably need a meat pounder, a round or rectangular flat piece of heavy metal with a handle, not to be confused with a toothy meat tenderizer. A weighty cleaver will also do the job.

Peeling vegetables goes faster with a swivel-bladed vegetable peeler, especially one with a fat, easy-grip handle. A clove of garlic inserted into a rubber tube called a garlic peeler makes short work of the skin with a quick back-and-forth motion. A rubber jar cap opener can be substituted. I rarely use a garlic press because it's a pain to clean. Chopping by hand or in a food processor is just as fast.

A salad spinner dries leafy greens more quickly than a colander and paper towels. Greens that are not particularly gritty (like romaine) can also be soaked in the spinner, rather than the sink, which saves even more time.

You should have a set of mixing bowls (ideally stainless steel), including one that is large enough for main-course salads. In a pinch, you can use a large pot.

To measure ingredients you'll need glass measuring cups for liquids, stainless steel measuring cups for dry ingredients, stainless steel measuring spoons, a ruler (to measure cut pieces of meat or vegetables), and a digital kitchen scale.

Other utensils to have on hand: a four-sided grater (for cheese and vegetables), a small colander or strainer for draining canned beans, a heavy-duty can opener, a timer (preferably magnetized), a hand juicer (the kind that looks like a sombrero and fits over a small bowl), a citrus zester, and a pepper mill (preferably one with different settings). I keep a potato masher, rubber spatulas, wooden spoons, wire whisks, a pasta fork, tongs (for turning meat), a wide metal spatula, solid and slotted spoons—and scratch-resistant versions of all—in a large wine bucket on the counter for easy access.

Freshly grated nutmeg is so superior to ground nutmeg that I no longer consider a nutmeg grater optional. But you may think otherwise. Other nice but not essential items include an egg cutter, which can be used to slice mushrooms, and a cocktail fork to extricate capers from a jar.

Having equipment within easy reach saves time. Because I use the food processor often, I keep it almost at arm's length. That avoids rattling around in the cupboard to look for it and the attachments. Whatever you use frequently should be immediately accessible and not require a foot stool or deep knee bends to find. Put the dim sum molds and other seldom-used gadgets in the back of a drawer or the far recesses of a cabinet.

FOCUS

Focus means being single-minded about getting the meal out in a hurry. It means the question, "How was your day, dear?" has to be asked and answered while eating dinner, not cooking it. No sipping of wine, listening to the news on the radio, or sifting through the mail. Get in there and get it done. Then be as leisurely as you want afterwards.

If there are two of you coming home at roughly the same time, one can cook while the other takes care of the kids and sets the table. The beauty of the recipes in this book is that they are designed for one person to cook. All the recipes have been tested to assure they can be completed in fifteen minutes. You may not be as experienced a cook as I am, or as familiar with the recipes. So on your first try a recipe may take fifteen to twenty minutes, maybe longer. However, once you get the hang of the concept, your speed will improve, sometimes dramatically. Pat Sinclair, one of my more ambitious testers, kept lowering her time with each of the recipes she tested. "I think I'm starting to get used to Sam's ways of doing things," she says. Larry Challacombe cooked the Braised Pork Tenderloin with Belgian Endive and Cranberry Relish (page 32) in nine minutes—faster than even I cooked the dish!

Some dishes don't require the cook to be working the entire time, as noted by Eileen Scheffel, who tested Snapper Veracruz (page 59). "Another thing I liked about this dish was that I had some 'free' time in the last six minutes while the fish cooked. I had the kitchen cleaned up and even had time to open a bottle of Corona and sit down for a minute before plating," she says.

Virtually all testers who took considerably more than fifteen minutes mentioned extenuating circumstances. Some professed being less than handy in the kitchen. Others didn't use time-saving equipment like a food processor for chopping because they didn't want to clean it. (I just pop mine in the dishwasher.) All this reminds me of what Arthur Schwartz told me when I was on his radio show in New York. "I have to have a glass of wine when I cook," he said. Fine, Arthur, as long as you are willing to cook for more than fifteen minutes.

Incidentally, the timing of these recipes begins when all ingredients and equipment are laid out and ready to go, what the French call *mis en place*. The buzzer sounds when the meal is ready to be dished out. It is assumed that all vegetables are washed except salad greens, which are cleaned within the fifteen minutes.

Read the entire recipe through before you start cooking. Most people know enough to get out the ingredients because they are listed at the top. But few read the method or text for what equipment is needed. You don't want to go searching for a pot in the middle of cooking, only to find it dirty in the dishwasher—or not find it at all.

Give yourself as much counter space as possible, even if it means putting a few things on the floor temporarily. My kitchen is so small that I routinely use the top of the refrigerator and microwave oven as holding areas.

Focus provides something even more important than speed—safety. Looking one way while performing a task in another direction is a recipe for injury. By being single-minded on the task at hand, you'll get it done quickly and safely. If there is ever a time when you think you are sacrificing safety for speed, *slow down*. Better to take an extra minute chopping that onion than lose the tip of your finger.

You'll notice that recipes will often say, "Meanwhile . . ." or "While the . . . cooks . . ." This lets you know that at the same time you are actively performing a task, something else is taking care of itself. For example, in the Beef and Beet Salad with Horseradish Cream Dressing (page 128), *four* things are going on at once. While the potatoes are boiling and the beef frying, the escarole is drying and the beets are draining.

You may be unaccustomed to managing such simultaneous tasks. However, soon you'll feel comfortable with the rhythm, which will make meal preparation more efficient and faster. At a charity event I attended in Wilmington, Delaware, Dave Anderson, chef of Iron Hill Brewery restaurant, told me that he makes his cooks read *Cooking to Beat the Clock* because it is so well organized.

I don't always indicate how an ingredient is supposed to look when it's done or ready for some other action—the way sautéed onion should look in a skillet when it's time to add wine, for instance. That's because you're cooking so quickly,

you don't always have the luxury of saying, "sauté the onions gently until they become a nice golden brown." Maybe on a leisurely Saturday afternoon, but not on Tuesday night at eight o'clock when you're famished. At other times, visual clues are given, such as tossing pasta until well coated with sauce.

The concept of focus also has a low-fat benefit I hadn't initially intended. Not having a glass of wine while cooking dinner eliminates those calories from alcohol. And without alcohol to stimulate the appetite, you're less likely to snack on fatty foods like nuts and cheese while you wait for dinner to be ready.

CREATIVITY

Creativity involves strategies for preparing meals in minutes, thinking beyond recipes so you don't always have to follow a specific formula. I realize that there is a certain comfort in following recipes. And I'm confident that the recipes in this book are good enough to be prepared again and again. Nevertheless, it's my hope that you'll use the recipes as a springboard, a blueprint if you will, to create many more fifteen-minute meals on your own.

To do this you need to think about concepts, rather than specific formulas. For example, Spicy Chicken and Broccoli Stir-Fry (page 43) is a meat-and-vegetable stir-fry when you break it down. If the meat isn't chicken, it could be turkey or pork tenderloin, or seafood, such as shrimp, scallops, or cubes of tuna or swordfish. In lieu of asparagus, vegetables might include string beans, broccoli, or several varieties of summer squash. Obviously, cooking times will vary, but you get the picture.

Similarly, the fillings in the Turkey Tacos with Red Pepper Salsa (page 49) or the Burritos with Braised Vegetables and Pumpkin Seeds (page 142) could be replaced with just about anything. Add an ingredient here and there if it happens to be in the fridge or you just feel like putting mango in the Warm Chicken Curry Salad (page 122). Maybe you want some red in the Pasta with Broccoli Raab and Feta Cheese (page 85). So you add some chopped roasted red bell pepper from a jar. Spices can change or vary in intensity to suit your particular taste. (See individual chapters for more examples of creativity.)

Creativity is especially important for low-fat cooking because you don't have the luxury of falling back on oils, butter, and other fatty ingredients to carry the day. You can't just throw the usual three parts oil to one part vinegar into a bowl for a salad vinaigrette because it blows your fat allotment sky high. That's where creativity comes in. To replace some of the oil, try fruit juices like lime, lemon, even orange. There are a plethora of vinegars from which to choose (see the Flavor section, page 16). There is also white wine, chicken or vegetable stock, and soy sauce. Or you could go creamy with nonfat yogurt, low-fat sour cream, or low-fat butter-milk. Don't think of it as an insurmountable obstacle but a welcome challenge, one you can more easily face with a well-stocked pantry and an organized kitchen.

Low-Fat and Quick-Cooking Tips

SHOPPING: Rather than writing a shopping list from scratch, keep a list of the usual pantry suspects in your computer, leaving enough space to write in special items. Print out the list before you go shopping and circle the items you need. If you don't have a computer, type or write the list by hand and make photocopies.

Make your list conform to the way your market is laid out. For example, at my store produce is in the front. So my list begins with produce. This will make shopping faster, and you'll be less likely to forget something. Write down items as they run out on a pad in the kitchen and refer to it when you make up your list.

To save money, buy the ends of the prosciutto for cooking. They don't make great slices but they're fine when cut into strips for dishes like Spaghetti Carbonara with Prosciutto and Peas (page 86).

To stay within the guideline of twelve grams of fat per serving, look for meats, fish, and poultry that are between five and ten grams of fat per serving. The remaining fat will come from cooking oil and other foods. (Vegetables, even herbs like mint, have some fat.)

STORING: To store fresh basil, try this neat trick I learned from my friend Janet Fletcher, author of *Fresh from the Farmers' Market*. Put a bunch of basil in a large plastic bag. Blow up the bag with air as you would a balloon and quickly secure the bag at the top with a twist tie. The basil will remain in pristine condition at room temperature for a week.

Despite conventional wisdom, keep onions and potatoes in the refrigerator. Storing onions under refrigeration eliminates tearing when they are chopped. The cold helps neutralize the volatile compounds that make us cry.

Refrigeration keeps potatoes away from light, which creates those toxic green blotches. The cold also keeps potatoes longer but it does affect their starch content. However, taking the potatoes out of the refrigerator a few hours before cooking—or perhaps before you leave for work—helps restabilize the starch.

MEATS: Don't have a meat pounder? Try a cast-iron skillet.

HERBS AND SPICES: Mail-order shopping (see page 149) is a good way to get herbs and spices not easily available from local stores. Herbs and spices purchased this way are also usually cheaper and fresher than those at supermarkets. If the amounts you order are more than you can reasonably use, consider splitting the spices and the cost with a friend who has similar culinary tastes.

Label dried herbs and spices with the purchase date so that you'll know when to replace them. When in doubt, take a sniff. If you can't smell anything, discard them.

For fresh ginger chopped by hand, first peel then cut the piece of ginger into thin slices or coins. Stack and cut the coins into strips. Cut the strips crosswise into small dice.

If you don't have a pepper mill with a coarse setting for dishes like Tuna Steak au Poivre with Buttermilk Mashed Potatoes (page 60), put peppercorns in a Ziploc bag and crush with a rolling pin or wine bottle.

To quickly remove the leaves from a sprig of tarragon or rosemary, hold the sprig in one hand about two-thirds up the stem and with the stem end down. Pull down toward the stem end with the closed thumb and forefinger of the other hand, stripping off the leaves. Then pick off the very top leaves.

SUBSTITUTING: Olives have a lot more fat than most people realize. Capers, which have no fat, can be substituted in many dishes. For example, my Couscous Salad (page 137) originally called for olives. But only ten kalamatas put the recipe over the twelve-gram fat limit per serving. Capers solved the dilemma.

MEASURING: While there is some flexibility in the use of seasonings and vegetables for the recipes in this book, cooking fats should be measured carefully. Similarly, cheese, meat, poultry, and fatty fish should be weighed on an accurate scale. Even when creating your own dish, get into the habit of always measuring fats.

CUTTING: When a recipe calls for a piece of meat or vegetable to be cut a certain size, measure one correct piece with a ruler. Put the piece at the top of the cutting board as your guide. Eyeball your sample piece periodically as you cut the rest of the pieces.

A cheese microplane is a grating tool based on a carpenter's wood rasp. It makes feathery curls of Parmesan, which cover more surface area on pasta than cheese grated conventionally. Thus, when diners add cheese at the table, they use less cheese and consume less fat.

COOKING: Lisa Callaghan of All-Clad Metalcrafters (which makes nonstick cookware) recommends using pump action rather than aerosol cooking sprays on nonstick cooking surfaces. Nonstick surfaces are not completely smooth, whether from the type of nonstick coating used, inevitable nicks and scratches, or food buildup you can't see because of the dark surface. Aerosol droplets from cooking sprays can get into these nooks and crannies. This can cause a sticky buildup and turn the normal blue-gray or black nonstick surface brown. Soaking the pan overnight in warm, soapy water, or scrubbing the surface with a sponge and a paste made of baking soda with a small amount of water can correct the problem. Better cookware stores sell pump spray canisters that can be filled with your own oil.

THE HOT TAP WATER ISSUE

As with *Cooking to Beat the Clock,* this book uses hot tap water to speed up cooking of rice, pasta, and vegetables. A few readers of my first book wrote to me and expressed concern that hot tap water contains substances that might be harmful. So I spoke to water authority Dr. James Symons, former Professor of Engineering at the University of Houston. Symons, known as Dr. Water because of his expertise in the field of H_2O, said he is not aware of any conclusive studies that indicate cooking with hot tap water is harmful. However, he said, "Because of the higher temperatures causing faster chemical reactions, hot water tends to be more corrosive than cold water. This means that impurities in the plumbing system, if any, could dissolve into the water more easily. Thus, for an added measure of safety, I recommend against using hot water for cooking or baby formula."

Food scientist Harold McGee, author of the acclaimed *On Food and Cooking,* wrote about cooking with hot tap water in the November 1995 issue of *Food & Wine* magazine. McGee told me that the hot tap water issue is "one of those annoyingly gray areas." He also said that it is less of a concern in more modern households where lead pipes have been replaced by copper or plastic, and unlined hot-water heaters have been replaced by those lined with fiberglass.

Unfortunately, there is no reliable test to determine whether or not the hot tap water in your home is appropriate for cooking. Flushing out the pipes by letting the water run doesn't mitigate any problem that may exist. If you have concerns about using hot tap water for cooking, use cold water, which will increase cooking times by a few minutes in the dishes affected.

Meat

Meat needn't be a rare occurrence on a low-fat diet. Pork has less fat than ever before. Veal and game are leaner still. Even beef provides cuts that are sufficiently low fat.

Three things must always be kept in mind, however. The first is portion control. I try to keep portions between four and six ounces (raw), and vary the portion depending on how much fat the meat contains. Thus, I can get away with five ounces of pork tenderloin in the Pork and Sweet Potato Stew with Couscous (page 31) because the meat has only one gram of fat per ounce or a total five grams of fat. Whereas I use four ounces of meat in the Beef Stroganoff (page 27) because the top round steak used in the recipe has 1.67 grams of fat per ounce or a total of 6.68 grams.

Regardless of the size of the portion, meat should be well-trimmed of external fat (the fat that surrounds the meat). The cuts I use for recipes are all in that category. Finally, be careful not to overcook these lean cuts because there is little internal fat to keep them moist. This is especially true of pork. We've been conditioned to cook pork to death in fear of trichinosis. But a little pink in the middle is advisable unless you particularly like the texture of cardboard.

One of my favorite low-fat meats is pork tenderloin, which has less fat than skinless dark meat chicken. Like chicken, it's quite versatile. In the Pork and Sweet Potato Stew with Couscous (page 31) it is cubed. In Braised Pork Tenderloin with Belgian Endive and Cranberry Relish (page 32), two tenderloins are halved. (Tenderloins generally weigh between ten and twenty ounces and often come two in a pack.) Tenderloins can also be cut into medallions, pounded, and sautéed like veal.

Other lean cuts for quick cooking include pork sirloin and top loin. Smithfield, known for its country hams, has a line of lean pork products called Smithfield Lean Generation, which are almost as low in fat as skinless chicken breasts. They can be ordered from retail stores or by mail order (see page 149).

The three main grades of beef are Prime, Choice, and Select. Prime has the most internal fat or marbling, Select has the least. Select has a tendency to be too lean, which is why many supermarkets are bringing back Choice. The nutrition analysis for beef recipes in this chapter uses well-trimmed Choice cuts. Over a quarter of all beef falls into the ungraded category, which may equate with Choice or Select. Ungraded beef is often sold under the store's brand, which may contain meaningless (and confusing) terms like Butcher's Prime. When in doubt, ask the butcher what the grade is and if the cut you're interested in is appropriate for the dish you want to cook.

The leanest cuts of beef are from the round—eye of the round, top round, and bottom round. Top round is often sold as London Broil and can be used for Beef and Beet Salad with Horseradish Cream Dressing (page 128) as well as Beef Stroganoff (see page 27). Some markets cut eye of the round into steaks. But even if cooked medium-rare they are chewy. A better choice is a sirloin tip steak or top sirloin steak. It's a little fattier but more tender and more like a steak in taste. This is the cut I use for Steak Diana with Skinny Jack Potatoes (page 28). After top sirloin the next leanest cuts are top loin and flank steak.

Veal, which comes from calves that are four months old or younger, is such a terrific low-fat meat that even untrimmed cuts aren't terribly fatty. For example, cutlets or scallopini cut from the leg, used in the Veal Marsala with Spinach and Shiitake Mushrooms (page 30) and Quick Blanquette de Veau (page 29), have .5 grams of fat per ounce if trimmed and .9 grams of fat if untrimmed. Loin and rib chops are also good cuts for low-fat quick cooking, as is calf's liver, for which I have a recipe in *Cooking to Beat the Clock*.

One of veal's drawbacks is its cost. For this reason I suggest using grass-fed or range-fed veal, which is less expensive than milk- or formula-fed veal, though a bit more difficult to find. This veal is reddish rather than pink and has a meatier flavor. It's also a bit chewier, though still plenty tender if cut from the leg. Because grass-fed or range-fed calves are allowed to roam, choosing meat from these animals eliminates another concern about veal. Some people object to milk- or formula-fed calves being cooped up in small pens without being able to move very much. If you've sworn off veal altogether, turkey breast is a good alternative for both veal recipes in this chapter.

Lamb is often thought of as a fatty meat, but it too has cuts that fit into a low-fat diet. An ounce of well-trimmed leg of lamb has only 1.3 grams of fat. Trimmed loin and rib chops have 1.7 and 2.6 grams of fat per ounce, respectively. New Zealand lamb, which is often available frozen, has slightly less fat than American lamb.

Game meats such as venison and buffalo are amazingly lean, so lean, in fact, that cuts that are to be grilled, broiled, or pan fried should be cooked no more than medium-rare or they will dry out. Venison, used in Venison with Port and Wild Mushrooms (page 35), is the most widely available of these meats. Here we're talking about farm-raised animals, often from New Zealand but increasingly from the United States. Unlike the twelve-point buck Uncle Harry shot, farm-raised venison has only a faintly gamy taste and is usually more tender. (See page 149 for mail-order sources.)

Whichever meat you use, season it well with salt and pepper before cooking. It's a myth that salt dries out meat. Salting before cooking makes meat taste better.

Beef Stroganoff

SERVES:	4	FAT:	8.8G /15.89%
CALORIES:	524.48	SATURATED FAT:	2.46G

Named after Count Paul Stroganoff, a member of the court of Tsar Alexander III, this dish harkens back to the '50s and '60s when most versions of this American favorite were heavy enough to sink the battleship Potemkin. But as James Beard once noted, stroganoff should not be a heavy stew but a lighter, quicker dish that can even be done tableside. It can also be made with veal, pork, or venison.

Canola oil spray
1 pound very lean round steak cut from the top round or bottom round
1½ teaspoons salt plus additional for seasoning
Freshly ground pepper
1 medium onion (about 8 ounces)
8 to 10 ounces button mushrooms
1½ tablespoons all-purpose flour
¼ cup dry sherry or brandy
¾ cup fat-free, reduced-sodium beef stock
One 8-ounce package of medium egg noodles or egg fettuccine
1 cup nonfat sour cream
1 tablespoon tomato paste
3 sprigs parsley, preferably flat-leaf

01 Run the hot-water tap and put 1½ quarts hot tap water in each of 2 pots (one large enough to eventually hold all the water and noodles). Cover and bring both pots to a boil over high heat, 7 to 9 minutes.

02 Meanwhile, spray a 12-inch, nonstick sauté pan with oil spray and put over medium heat. Cut the steak in half lengthwise, then cut crosswise into thin strips about 1½ inches long and ½ inch wide. Season with salt and pepper and add to the pan. Raise the heat to high and cook for 3 minutes, stirring once or twice to brown evenly.

03 Meanwhile, cut off a thin slice from the top and bottom of the onion, halve lengthwise, peel each half, and cut them crosswise into ¼-inch-thick half-moon slices. Thinly slice the mushrooms. Remove the beef to a platter and add the onion and mushrooms to the pan. Season with salt and pepper. Cook for 2 minutes, stirring once or twice. Sprinkle with the flour and cook for 1 minute, stirring well. Add the sherry and beef stock. Mix well and bring to a boil, then reduce heat to a simmer.

04 When the water for the noodles boils, transfer the water from the smaller pot to the larger pot. Add the 1½ teaspoons of salt to the larger pot and add the noodles. Cook for 5 minutes, or until the noodles are firm but tender. Drain.

05 While the noodles cook, mix the sour cream and tomato paste in a small bowl. Chop the parsley leaves. Return the beef to the pan and add the sour cream mixture. Stir well to incorporate. Do not boil. Cook for a few minutes or until completely heated through. Serve over the noodles, sprinkled with the chopped parsley.

Steak Diana with Skinny Jack Potatoes

SERVES: 4
CALORIES: 358.30
FAT: 11.14G /30.40%
SATURATED FAT: 4.87G

This low-fat version of the showy restaurant classic is easily re-created at home. Sirloin tip or top sirloin steaks can be found in most markets these days. In my market the cut is labeled "beef round sirloin tip" and weighs about two-thirds of a pound. (So I use two steaks for four servings.) Because this cut is so lean, I advise cooking it medium-rare. The potatoes are a slimmed-down adaptation of a recipe by master chef Jacques Pepin.

Canola oil spray
1 pound bag frozen (uncooked)
    hash-brown potatoes
1¼ cups 2-percent milk
2 cloves garlic
Salt
Freshly ground pepper
4 top sirloin steaks, 4 to 5 ounces each
2 small to medium shallots or 1 large
3 to 4 sprigs parsley, preferably flat-leaf,
    enough for 1 to 1½ tablespoons when chopped
⅓ cup Cognac or good brandy
½ cup fat-free, reduced-sodium beef stock
1 tablespoon unsalted butter

01 Spray a large, heavy-bottomed saucepan with canola oil spray. Put the potatoes and milk in the saucepan, cover, and put over medium-high heat. Peel and chop the garlic. Add the garlic to the potatoes. Season to taste with salt and pepper. Stir and cover. When the milk begins to boil (2 to 3 minutes), reduce the heat to medium and cook, partially covered, for about 10 minutes, stirring periodically, or until the liquid has been absorbed and the potatoes are still moist and creamy.

02 Meanwhile, spray a 10-inch, cast-iron or other large, heavy skillet with canola oil spray and put over high heat. Season the steaks with salt and pepper. Add the steaks to the skillet and cook for 2 minutes. While the steaks cook, peel and chop the shallots. Chop the parsley leaves. Turn the steaks over and cook for 2 minutes.

03 When the steaks are cooked on both sides, remove the skillet from the heat and add the brandy. Making sure not to lean over the skillet, ignite the liquor with a match, preferably a long fireplace-type match. The flames will shoot up briefly and die down quickly. Have a skillet cover handy just in case you need to put out the flames.

04 When the flames subside, put the skillet over high heat and turn the steaks to coat both sides. Remove the steaks to a platter and cover with aluminum foil. Add the stock and shallots to the skillet and cook for 2 minutes, or until the sauce begins to reduce and thicken slightly. Reduce the heat to medium and swirl in the butter. Stir the parsley into the potatoes and pour into a bowl. Put the steaks on individual plates and pour the sauce over them. Serve with the potatoes.

Quick Blanquette de Veau

SERVES:	4	FAT:	7.56g /14.09%
CALORIES:	482.86	SATURATED FAT:	.84g

The traditional blanquette involves poaching tough cubes of veal shoulder for over an hour until tender, then enriching the dish with eggs and cream at the end. We can't afford the time or calories for either. So I've modified the recipe by using more tender veal cutlets and substituting evaporated skim milk for the cream and eggs. You can cut the cost—and a few calories—by reducing the amount of veal to one pound. For convenience, use frozen peas and pearl onions packaged together.

1 cup basmati rice

1 teaspoon salt plus additional for seasoning

Olive oil spray

1¼ pounds veal cutlets or veal scallopini

Freshly ground pepper

One 10-ounce package of frozen peas with
   pearl onions

6 ounces mushrooms

1 tablespoon olive oil

2 tablespoons all-purpose flour

2 teaspoons fresh thyme or ¾ teaspoon dried

⅓ cup dry white wine

¾ cup fat-free, reduced-sodium chicken stock

½ cup pimiento or roasted red bell pepper
   from a jar

One 5-ounce can evaporated skim milk

01 While the hot-water tap runs, put the rice in a 2-quart saucepan. Add 2 cups hot tap water and the 1 teaspoon salt. Cover and bring to a boil over high heat. Reduce the heat to low and cook for 10 minutes. Turn the heat off and keep covered until ready to serve. (Or put the rice, 2 cups hot tap water, and the 1 teaspoon salt in a 2-quart, microwave-safe container. Cover and cook in a microwave oven on high power for 10 minutes. Keep covered until ready to serve.)

02 Meanwhile, spray a 12-inch, nonstick sauté pan with olive oil spray and put over medium heat. Cut the veal into strips about 1 inch long and ½ inch wide. Season with salt and pepper and add to the sauté pan. Raise the heat to high and stir.

03 Put the peas and onions in a colander and run hot tap water over them while you thinly slice the mushrooms. Remove the veal and any accumulated juices to a bowl. Add the olive oil, mushrooms, and salt to taste to the sauté pan. Lower the heat to medium-high, stir, and cook for 2 minutes. Sprinkle with flour and cook for 1 minute, stirring a few times. Add the thyme, wine, and chicken stock and stir well. Add the peas and onions and raise the heat to high. Stir to mix well, cover, and bring to a boil.

04 Meanwhile, chop the pimiento or roasted pepper into approximately ¼-inch pieces. Add to the sauté pan with the evaporated milk and cover. As soon as the mixture returns to a boil (a minute or less), uncover and return the veal and its juices to the pan. Bring to a brisk simmer while stirring constantly to prevent the sauce from separating. Cook until sauce thickens slightly, about 2 or 3 minutes. Serve the veal over the rice.

Veal Marsala with Spinach and Shiitake Mushrooms

SERVES: 4	FAT: 9.62g /29.60%
CALORIES: 320.94	SATURATED FAT: 2.36g

This recipe works best in a pan without a nonstick surface. Bits of the veal's flour coating stick to the pan and are loosened when Marsala and chicken stock are added. These particles flavor and thicken the sauce. Cutlets or scallopini usually come in 2- to 3-ounce pieces. Thus, you'll need 6 to 8 cutlets, which will have to be cooked in 2 batches. However, scallopini only take a minute to cook on each side. Don't forget to drink the juice left over from cooking the spinach. It's delicious.

Canola or olive oil spray

¼ pound shiitake or button mushrooms

1 medium shallot

Two 10-ounce bags of cleaned fresh spinach

1½ tablespoons olive oil

16 to 20 ounces of veal cutlets or scallopini
   (6 to 8 pieces)

Salt

Freshly ground pepper

⅓ cup all-purpose flour for dredging

¼ teaspoon ground nutmeg, preferably
   freshly grated

½ tablespoon butter

½ cup Marsala wine or sweet vermouth

¼ cup fat-free, reduced-sodium chicken stock

01 Spray a 12-inch, nonstick sauté pan or Dutch oven with oil spray and put over medium heat. Remove the stems from the shiitake mushrooms (if using button mushrooms, leave the stems on) and thinly slice the caps. Peel and chop the shallot. Add the mushrooms and shallot to the pan. Increase the heat to medium-high. Stir, cover, and cook for 2 minutes. Meanwhile, put the spinach into a large colander; pick through and discard any thick stems or damaged leaves. Rinse briefly and put the spinach into the pan with the mushrooms and shallots. Cover the pan.

02 Put the olive oil in a 12-inch, heavy skillet over high heat. Season half the cutlets with salt and pepper. Put the flour on a sheet of wax paper or in a pie plate. Dredge the seasoned cutlets in the flour, shaking off any excess. Put the seasoned and floured veal in the skillet and cook for 1 minute on each side. Meanwhile, season and flour the remaining cutlets. Transfer the cooked cutlets to a platter and cover with aluminum foil. Add the next batch of cutlets and cook for 1 minute on each side. Add to the platter.

03 While the veal cooks, season the spinach with the nutmeg and salt and pepper to taste. Add the butter and stir well. Turn off the heat when the spinach is just wilted.

04 When all the veal has been cooked, add the Marsala and stock to the skillet and bring to a boil over high heat, scraping the bottom of the pan with a wooden spoon to release any food particles. Return the veal to the pan and coat with the sauce for about 30 seconds. Then put the veal back on the platter and spoon the sauce over as soon as it begins to thicken, which should be almost immediately. Serve the veal with the spinach.

Pork and Sweet Potato Stew with Couscous

SERVES: 4

CALORIES: 642.40

FAT: 11.10g /15.71%

SATURATED FAT: 3.13g

This is a kind of tagine, the stew so popular in North Africa, though in that part of the world it would be made with lamb, chicken, seafood, or vegetables since many North Africans are Muslims who shun pork. Despite its exotic origins, the ingredients in this dish are easily available in most supermarkets.

Olive or canola oil spray

Two 10-ounce pork tenderloins

2 large sweet potatoes (about 2 pounds total)

1 tablespoon ground ginger

1 teaspoon ground coriander

½ teaspoon salt plus additional for seasoning

Freshly ground pepper

2 cups fat-free, reduced-sodium chicken stock

1¼ cups instant couscous

12 small (or 6 large) dried apricots

2 tablespoons sesame seeds

01 Spray a 12-inch, nonstick sauté pan or Dutch oven with olive oil spray and put over medium heat. Beginning at the thick end, cut the pork into ½-inch-thick slices, increasing the thickness to about 1 inch as you move toward the thinner end. Add the pork to the skillet. Increase the heat to high and stir.

02 Peel and halve the sweet potatoes lengthwise. Cut the potatoes into thin half-moon slices and add them to the pan. (Or slice the potatoes using the slicing attachment of a food processor.) Add the ginger, coriander, and salt and pepper to taste. Stir well. Add the chicken stock, cover, and bring to a boil.

03 Meanwhile, run the hot-water tap and put 1¼ cups hot water and the ½ teaspoon salt in a 2-quart saucepan. Put over high heat, cover, and bring to a boil, about 3 minutes. (Or put the couscous, the ½ teaspoon salt, and 1¼ cups hot water in a microwave-safe container. Cover and cook on high power for 6 minutes.)

04 While the water for the couscous comes to a boil, slice the apricots and add to the stew. Reduce the heat under the stew to medium-high. Cook, covered, until the potatoes are just tender, about 8 minutes, stirring once or twice. When the couscous water comes to a boil, add the couscous, stir, and turn off the heat. Cover and let the couscous steam for 7 minutes. (If using the microwave, also let the couscous steam for 7 minutes.)

05 While the couscous steams, toast the sesame seeds in a cast-iron skillet over medium heat for 3 minutes. Spoon the couscous onto a large, deep platter making a shallow well in the middle. With a slotted spoon, put the pork and sweet potatoes into the well. Then spoon the broth over the pork, sweet potatoes, and couscous. Sprinkle with the sesame seeds.

Braised Pork Tenderloin with
Belgian Endive and Cranberry Relish

SERVES: 4	FAT: 8.26g /16.34%
CALORIES: 442.02	SATURATED FAT: 2.69g

My fondness for cranberry sauce goes well beyond Thanksgiving, so I freeze bags of cranberries for the winter. Cranberry sauce is a great accompaniment to many meat dishes, especially pork and game. (Try it with the Venison with Port and Wild Mushrooms on page 35.) If you like your cranberry relish a bit tart, use ¾ cup of sugar instead of 1 cup. Instead of Belgian endive, my wife, Mary, prefers this dish with Skinny Jack Potatoes (page 28) or Buttermilk Mashed Potatoes (page 60) to soak up the pan juices.

Canola oil spray
2 pork tenderloins (about 10 ounces each)
Salt
Freshly ground pepper
Four 4-ounce Belgian endives
1 large shallot
¾ cup fat-free, reduced-sodium chicken stock
2 tablespoons candied (crystallized) ginger
1 small juice orange
One 12-ounce bag fresh or frozen cranberries
¼ to 1 cup sugar
3 sprigs parsley, preferably flat-leaf
Paprika for garnishing

01 Spray a 12-inch, nonstick skillet with canola oil spray and put over medium heat. Cut each tenderloin in half lengthwise. Fold up an inch or more of the narrow portion of the tenderloin and secure it to the fatter portion with a toothpick. Season with salt and pepper. Add to the skillet and raise heat to high.

02 Cut off ½ inch from the stem end of each endive and place around the pork in the skillet. Season the endives with salt and pepper to taste. Peel and mince the shallot. Turn over the pork and the endives and cook for 1 minute

03 Add the stock to the skillet and sprinkle the shallot over the pork and endive. Cover and bring to a boil. Reduce the heat to medium and cook for 8 minutes or just until endive is tender and the pork is light pink inside. Check the skillet once to make sure the endives and tenderloins are cooking evenly.

04 Meanwhile, drop the ginger down the chute of a food processor with the motor running. When the ginger is chopped, turn off the motor. Quarter the orange and remove the white membrane in the middle and any pits. Do not peel. Add the orange to the food processor and pulse until coarsely chopped. Scrape down the sides of the bowl with a rubber spatula. Add the cranberries and sugar. (If the cranberries are frozen, put them in a colander and run them under hot water for 30 to 60 seconds, while tossing them gently to defrost evenly.) Pulse until well combined. Scrape down the sides of the bowl halfway through with a rubber spatula. Pour into a serving bowl.

05 Chop the parsley leaves. Put the pork and endive on individual plates or a platter and increase the heat in the sauté pan to high to reduce the sauce slightly. Pour the sauce over the pork and endive. Sprinkle with the parsley and paprika. Serve with the cranberry relish.

Pork Chops with Cabbage and Apples

SERVES:	4	FAT:	9.72g /27.82%
CALORIES:	361.01	SATURATED FAT:	3.22g

I love cabbage, pork, and apples cooked almost any way. Here you can vary most, if not all, the ingredients to suit taste, even color. For example, you could use red cabbage and a tart green apple like Granny Smith instead of green cabbage and red apples. Other seasonings could be ginger, nutmeg, cloves, cinnamon, even pumpkin pie seasoning. Using already shredded cabbage makes things easier.

Canola oil spray
Four 5-ounce boneless loin center-cut pork chops
1 teaspoon ground allspice
Salt
1 medium onion (about 8 ounces)
1¼ pounds cabbage
1 large, tart red apple such as winesap
2 teaspoons caraway seeds
Freshly ground pepper
1¼ cups off-dry white wine such as Riesling
**   or Gewürztraminer**
¼ cup red wine vinegar
¼ teaspoon ground cloves
1 tablespoon sugar

01 Spray a nonstick skillet with canola oil spray and put over medium heat. Season the pork with allspice and salt and add to the skillet. Cover.

02 Meanwhile, spray a 12-inch, nonstick sauté pan or Dutch oven with canola oil spray and put over medium heat. Peel and quarter the onion. Put the onion in a food processor and pulse just until chopped. (Or chop by hand.) Add to the sauté pan, increase the heat to medium-high, and stir. Remove the core from the cabbage and shred using a chef's knife, the large holes of a four-sided grater, or the slicing attachment of the food processor. Add to the onion, stir, and cover. Turn the chops over.

03 Sit the apple upright on a cutting board and cut straight down on four sides around the core. (Do not peel.) Cut the sides into ½-inch cubes and add to the cabbage and onion. Add the caraway seeds and salt and pepper to taste. Stir well.

04 Put the chops on top of the cabbage mixture and cover. Mix the wine, wine vinegar, cloves, and sugar in a small bowl. Pour over the pork and cabbage. Cover and cook for 5 minutes, or until the cabbage is wilted but still firm and the pork chops are cooked through. Shake the pan a few times to cook evenly. If some liquid remains when the cabbage is done, spoon it over the pork when serving.

Venison with Port and Wild Mushrooms

SERVES: 4
CALORIES: 417.04
FAT: 7.60g / 18.02%
SATURATED FAT: 3.27g

Save this low-fat meal for a special occasion because venison isn't cheap. But it's worth it, according to tester C. R. Griffin, Jr. "Awesome—a true hit," he says. Venison is extremely lean. So don't cook the meat more than medium-rare or you'll have expensive shoe leather. This is a good time to break out that serious red wine you've been cellaring. (Griffin tried it with an 11-year-old California Cabernet Sauvignon.)

2 pounds parsnips
One 20-ounce loin of venison or two smaller loins, 10 ounces each, or a 1½-pound rack of venison containing 4 chops
Salt
Freshly ground pepper
Canola oil spray
½ pound small to medium mushrooms
1 shallot
½ cup Port wine
½ cup fat-free, reduced-sodium beef stock
8 chives
1 tablespoon butter

01 Turn on the broiler and put a 10-inch, cast-iron skillet about 5 inches from the heat source.

02 Peel the parsnips. While the hot-water tap runs, halve them lengthwise, then cut crosswise into thin slices as uniformly as possible, by hand or using the slicing attachment of a food processor. Put the parsnips in a microwave-safe container with ⅓ cup of hot tap water. Cover and cook in a microwave oven on high power for 10 minutes, or until just tender, shaking the container once during cooking. (Or put the parsnips in a deep skillet or wide saucepan and barely cover with hot tap water. Cover and cook over high heat for 10 minutes or until just tender.)

03 Meanwhile, if using one large loin, cut crosswise into 4 pieces of roughly equal size. If using two loins, halve them crosswise. If using a rack of venison, cut into 4 chops. Season the meat with the salt and pepper, spray with canola oil, and rub in the seasonings. Put the venison in the hot skillet from the broiler and return the skillet to the broiler for 3 to 4 minutes, 2 to 3 minutes for chops.

04 While the venison cooks, spray a 12-inch, nonstick skillet with canola oil spray and put over medium heat. Slice the mushrooms. Peel and chop the shallot. Increase the heat under the skillet to high and add the shallot and mushrooms. Add salt and pepper to taste and cook for 4 minutes, stirring once or twice. Meanwhile, turn the venison over and cook for another 3 to 4 minutes for medium-rare (2 to 3 minutes for chops).

05 Add the Port and stock to the mushrooms and cook for 2 to 3 minutes. Meanwhile, chop the chives. Drain the parsnips, reserving 2 tablespoons of the cooking liquid. Toss the parsnips with the cooking liquid, chives, butter, and salt and pepper to taste. Divide among four plates. Put the venison on the plates and spoon the mushroom sauce over the meat.

Poultry

Unless you've been living on one of Jupiter's moons for the last twenty years, you probably know that removing the skin from poultry significantly reduces the fat content. An ounce of chicken breast meat without skin has only .4 grams of fat. With skin, it jumps to 2.6 grams.

Boneless and skinless chicken breasts are also extremely versatile, whether whole, in dishes such as Chicken à la Moutarde (page 46) and Chicken in Vinegar Sauce with Chived Potatoes (page 39), or cut up in dishes like Spicy Chicken and Broccoli Stir-Fry (page 43). Despite this flexibility, boneless chicken breasts can become a bit boring, so I jazz things up occasionally by leaving the meat on the bone, as in Pan-Roasted Chicken Breast with Lima Bean Puree (page 44). This will keep chicken more moist and flavorful, though it will take a little longer to cook and require some care to avoid the bones when eating.

Cooking goes faster if the breasts are pounded to half their original thickness. Many supermarkets now offer skinless and boneless breasts that way. For breasts on the bone, have a butcher do the pounding. Or do it at home. It's a simple task. Some supermarkets also offer chicken tenders, boneless chicken breasts cut into thick strips. Tenders can be cut into cubes for stir-fries like Spicy Chicken and Broccoli Stir-Fry (page 43), or they can also be used for chicken fajitas.

Chicken thighs have only 1.2 grams of fat per ounce, and their richer, meatier flavor lends them to hearty dishes like Chicken Cacciatore (page 48). The disadvantage is that thighs are rarely sold off the bone. Boning takes time, so I prefer to whack thighs in half (through the bone) with a cleaver to create smaller pieces for speedier cooking.

Free-range chickens—birds allowed to roam instead of being cooped up—often provide superior tasting meat, usually with less fat. For these reasons, you may be willing to pay the extra money they cost. Kosher chickens are also more flavorful (and more expensive) because they are salted or put into a brine solution.

Turkey has a deeper flavor than chicken but with a comparable amount of fat. Turkey cutlets are slices of boneless turkey breast meat which can be used in sautéed dishes the same as pounded chicken breasts. They are also an alternative to veal cutlets in sautéed veal dishes like Veal Marsala with Spinach and Shiitake Mushrooms (page 30). Or they can be cut into strips for fajitas or taco fillings, as in Turkey Tacos with Red Pepper Salsa (page 49).

In an effort to avoid salmonella, consumers tend to overcook poultry. This poses a greater problem in low-fat cooking because there is no skin and less cooking fat to keep the meat moist. Chicken and turkey are done the moment all pink disappears and should not be cooked a moment longer, though there is a bit of a cushion with dark meat. When in doubt, cut into a breast with a sharp paring knife to determine doneness.

Ground turkey and chicken meat provide worthy alternatives to ground beef for dishes such as chili and hearty pasta ragus like Spaghetti Squash with Turkey Bolognese Sauce (page 53). But unless the package says "ground breast meat," you're likely to get white meat, dark meat, and some skin thrown in for good measure. So read the labels.

Most low-fat cookbooks tell you to avoid duck because it has so much fat. But almost all of that fat is in the skin, which is easily stripped away from the breast. Skinless duck breast has only 1.7 grams of fat per ounce. Duck breast should be cooked no more than medium, preferably medium-rare, to avoid toughness. (Salmonella is less of an issue with duck than with chicken or turkey.) After cooking, the meat should rest, even if only for a few minutes to relax the fibers, which tighten during cooking. Duck isn't cheap, but a full breast (two halves) is usually enough for four people, as in the Asian Duck Salad (page 55). More markets are selling duck breasts separately, though they can also be ordered by mail (see page 149).

Game birds are lean and flavorful alternatives to turkey and chicken, and they have become more widely available in recent years. Quail is probably the most accessible and is a good choice for quick pan frying, broiling, and grilling.

Even when you're in a rush to get dinner on the table, it's important to avoid contamination from raw poultry. I usually keep raw poultry separated from my cutting board by working with it on the wrapping paper in which it came. If I do use the cutting board, I'll wash it when I clean other contaminated surfaces, like hands and knives, with hot, soapy water, which I have close by in a small plastic bucket.

Chicken in Vinegar Sauce with Chived Potatoes

SERVES:	4	FAT:	8.88g / 20.09%
CALORIES:	403.01	SATURATED FAT:	2.82g

Chicken sautéed with vinegar may sound odd, but vinegar has lots of flavor, especially sherry vinegar and well-made wine vinegars. And they're fat free, of course. If you like, substitute fresh herbs such as thyme, basil, or rosemary for herbes de Provence. Larger potatoes cut into large cubes can be used in place of small new potatoes. Use the white part of 6 green onions to replace the shallots and the green part to replace the chives, if you wish.

1½ pounds small new potatoes (12 to 16)

1 teaspoon salt plus additional for seasoning

1 tablespoon extra-virgin olive oil

Four 6-ounce boneless and skinless chicken
    breasts pounded flat (by the butcher if possible)
    to half their original thickness

Freshly ground pepper

3 shallots

8 to 10 chives

3 sprigs parsley, preferably flat-leaf

1 ripe medium to large tomato (8 to 12 ounces)
    or 1 cup drained, canned diced tomatoes

¼ cup sherry vinegar or red wine vinegar

¼ cup fat-free, reduced-sodium chicken stock

1 teaspoon herbes de Provence or equal amounts
    of dried thyme and marjoram or rosemary

1 tablespoon butter

01 While the hot-water tap runs, halve the potatoes and put in a 2-quart saucepan. Barely cover them with hot tap water and put over high heat. Add the 1 teaspoon salt, cover, and cook for 13 minutes or until easily pierced with a knife. (Or put the potatoes, the ¼ cup hot tap water, and the 1 teaspoon salt in a microwave-safe container. Cover and cook in a microwave oven on high power for 10 minutes or until easily pierced with a knife.)

02 Meanwhile, put the olive oil in a 12-inch, nonstick sauté pan over medium heat. Season both sides of each chicken breast with salt and pepper. (If the butcher hasn't done so, pound the chicken between two sheets of aluminum foil or plastic wrap with the side of a cleaver or a meat pounder before seasoning.) Put the chicken in the skillet, increase the heat to high, and cook for 4 minutes.

03 Meanwhile, peel the shallots and put in a food processor. Pulse until chopped. (Or chop by hand.) Chop the chives. Chop the parsley leaves. Core and chop the tomato.

04 Turn the chicken breasts over and add the shallots to the pan. Shake to distribute evenly. Cook for 1 minute. Add the vinegar and chicken stock. Stir well with a wooden spoon. Add the tomatoes and herbes de Provence. Cover and cook for 3 minutes or until the chicken shows no pink inside. (Cut into one piece to check if you're not sure.) Shake the pan a few times to distribute ingredients evenly.

05 As soon as the potatoes are done, drain and toss with the butter, chives, and salt and pepper to taste. Put the potatoes in a small serving bowl. Put the chicken on a serving platter, pour the sauce from the pan over it, and sprinkle with the chopped parsley.

Moroccan Lemon Chicken

| SERVES: | 4 | FAT: | 10.68g /15.12% |
| CALORIES: | 642.48 | SATURATED FAT: | 1.86g |

This is a quicker, low-fat version of a recipe from *Matthew Kenney's Mediterranean Cooking,* which I wrote with Matthew Kenney. It is indicative of the intense flavors Matthew brings to his food, and shows how you can still have most of those flavors while reducing the fat.

Olive oil spray

Four 5- to 6-ounce boneless and skinless chicken
    breast halves, pounded flat (by the butcher if possible)
    to half their original thickness

½ teaspoon salt plus additional for seasoning

Freshly ground black pepper

¼ cup pine nuts or slivered almonds

1¼ cups instant couscous

4 cloves garlic

One 2-inch piece fresh ginger

1 medium to large onion (8 to 12 ounces)

½ cup pitted green olives or pimiento-stuffed green olives

1 lemon

2 tablespoons honey

¼ teaspoon saffron threads

Healthy pinch of cayenne pepper

1 cup fat-free, reduced-sodium chicken stock

01 Spray a 12-inch, nonstick sauté pan with olive oil spray and put over medium heat. Season the chicken with salt and black pepper. (If the butcher hasn't done so, pound the chicken between two sheets of aluminum foil or plastic wrap with the side of a cleaver or a meat pounder before seasoning.) Put the chicken in the pan. Increase the heat to medium-high, and brown on one side for 4 minutes.

02 Meanwhile, turn the oven to 500 degrees F. Put the pine nuts or almonds on a pie plate and put in the oven. Toast 8 to 10 minutes or until browned, shaking the pan a few times to toast evenly. Run the hot-water tap and put 1¾ cups hot tap water and the ½ teaspoon salt in a 2-quart saucepan over high heat. Cover and bring to a boil, about 3 minutes. (Or put the couscous, the ½ teaspoon salt, and 1¾ cups hot water in a microwave-safe container. Cover and cook on high power for 6 minutes.)

03 Peel the garlic and ginger. Cut the ginger in half. With the motor of a food processor running, drop the garlic and ginger down the chute and finely chop. Turn the chicken breasts over. Peel the onion, quarter, and add to the garlic and ginger. Pulse until just chopped. (Or chop by hand.)

04 When the water in the saucepan comes to a boil, add the couscous, stir, and turn off the heat. Cover and let the couscous steam for 7 minutes. (If using the microwave, also let the couscous steam for 7 minutes.) Remove the chicken to a platter. Add the garlic, ginger, and onion to the pan and stir.

05 Coarsely chop the olives. Juice the lemon. Add the olives, lemon juice, honey, saffron, cayenne, and stock to the pan and increase the heat to high. Return the chicken to the pan and add the toasted pine nuts. Mix well, cover, and bring to a boil. Reduce the heat and simmer for 4 to 5 minutes, or until the chicken shows no pink in the center. (Cut into one piece to check if you're not sure.) Put the couscous in 4 individual soup plates, put the chicken on top of the couscous, and pour the sauce over.

Spicy Chicken and Broccoli Stir-Fry

SERVES: 4	**FAT:** 6.27g /13.18%
CALORIES: 426.86	**SATURATED FAT:** 1.07g

There is a delightful sweet and hot melody to this dish. However, if you're more sensitive to hot food than I am, you might cut back on the red pepper flakes or cayenne. Pre-cut broccoli florets, which many supermarkets now carry in their produce sections or on their salad bars, help to speed things up. Some markets have broccoli crowns, essentially small heads of broccoli with no stems. Crowns can then be broken up into florets.

1 cup basmati rice
1 teaspoon salt plus additional for seasoning
1 head broccoli (about 1 pound) or 1 pound
    broccoli florets or crowns
3 cloves garlic
One 2-inch piece fresh ginger
2 tablespoons dry sherry or rice wine
2 tablespoons hoisin sauce
1 tablespoon soy sauce
1 teaspoon red pepper flakes or cayenne pepper
1 tablespoon peanut or canola oil
1¼ pounds boneless and skinless chicken
    breasts or chicken tenders
½ cup fat-free, reduced-sodium chicken stock
2 teaspoons cornstarch
One 8-ounce can sliced water chestnuts

01   While the hot-water tap runs, put the rice in a 2-quart saucepan. Add 2 cups hot tap water and the 1 teaspoon salt. Cover and bring to a boil over high heat. Reduce the heat to low and cook for 10 minutes. Turn the heat off and keep covered until ready to serve. (Or put the rice, 2 cups hot tap water, and the 1 teaspoon salt in a 2-quart, microwave-safe container. Cover and cook in a microwave oven on high power for 10 minutes. Keep covered until ready to serve.)

02   Meanwhile, cut the bottom 1 inch from the stem of a head of broccoli. Separate the stem from the head. Peel the stem and cut crosswise into ¼-inch-thick slices. Separate the heads into florets. Set aside.

03   Peel the garlic. Peel and halve the ginger. With the motor of a food processor running, drop the garlic and ginger down the chute and finely chop. Turn off the motor and scrape down the sides of the bowl with a rubber spatula. Add the sherry, hoisin, soy, and red pepper flakes. Leave the ingredients in the food processor.

04   Put the oil in a wok or a 12-inch, nonstick sauté pan over medium-low heat. Cut the chicken into 1-inch cubes. Raise the heat under the pan to high. Add the chicken, season with salt, and stir. Add the broccoli and cook for 3 minutes, stirring periodically. Meanwhile, mix the chicken stock and cornstarch in a cup. Add to the food processor and turn on the machine while you open and drain the can of water chestnuts.

05   Add the sauce and water chestnuts to the pan. Stir well and cook for 2 minutes, or until the chicken and broccoli are cooked through and the sauce is lightly thickened. (Add a bit more chicken stock or water if the broccoli and chicken aren't done when the sauce has thickened.) Serve over the rice.

Pan-Roasted Chicken Breast with Lima Bean Puree

SERVES: 4	FAT: 9.98g /18.68%
CALORIES: 493.69	SATURATED FAT: 3.10g

In *Cooking to Beat the Clock*, Chicks and Bricks was my take on the Tuscan *pollo al mattone*, chicken weighed down with foil-wrapped bricks so it cooks quickly with a crisp skin. My low-fat version has no skin but is delicious nonetheless. Actually, you don't really need bricks to make the dish work. An enameled cast-iron Dutch oven or similar heavy pot sitting on a sheet of foil works even better because it's easier to remove.

1 tablespoon olive oil

1 pound bag frozen baby lima beans

2 teaspoons salt

½ teaspoon freshly ground black pepper

¼ teaspoon cayenne pepper

4 skinless chicken breast halves on the bone, about 12 ounces each, pounded flat (by the butcher if possible) to half their original thickness

5 sprigs fresh rosemary or 1 teaspoon dried

4 chives or 3 sprigs parsley, preferably flat-leaf

1 tablespoon butter

01 Put the olive oil in a heavy, 12-inch skillet over medium heat.

02 While the hot-water tap runs, put the lima beans in a wide saucepan. Add 1½ cups hot tap water and put the saucepan over high heat. Add 1 teaspoon of the salt, cover, and cook for 5 minutes.

03 Meanwhile, mix the remaining 1 teaspoon of salt, black pepper, and cayenne in a small bowl. Season the fleshy part of the chicken with half of the spice mixture. (If the butcher hasn't done so, pound the chicken between two sheets of aluminum foil or plastic wrap with the side of a cleaver or a meat pounder before seasoning.)

04 Increase the heat under the skillet to high. Put the chicken in the skillet, fleshy side down. Season the other side of the chicken with the remaining half of the spice mixture and cover with foil. Put a Dutch oven or similar heavy pot weighing at least 5 pounds on top of the foil. Cook for 5 minutes. Reduce the heat under the lima beans to medium-high and cook for 8 minutes more or until the beans are just tender.

05 While the chicken and lima beans cook, chop the leaves from one of the rosemary sprigs. You should have about 2 teaspoons. (Save the other sprigs for garnish.) Chop the chives or the parsley leaves. Turn the chicken over and put the foil and weight back in place. Lower the heat to medium-high and cook for 5 minutes or until no pink shows in the meat. (Cut into one piece to check if you're not sure.)

06 When the lima beans are done, put them and their cooking liquid in a food processor with the chopped rosemary and butter. Pulse just until pureed, scraping down the sides of the bowl to fully incorporate the mixture. Add a little hot tap water if needed to make a smooth puree. Put the chicken breasts on 4 individual plates. Divide the bean puree among the plates and garnish each by sticking a rosemary sprig in the puree like a flag.

Chicken à la Moutarde

SERVES: 4	**FAT:** 7.68g /16.57%
CALORIES: 477.21	**SATURATED FAT:** 1.46g

This is a variation of the French bistro favorite, *lapin à la moutarde,* rabbit with mustard sauce. The mustard not only adds flavor but thickens the sauce without butter or flour. And by using a tarragon or herbes de Provence—flavored Dijon, you don't need any other seasoning except salt, pepper, and a sprinkling of parsley. If you can't find the flavored mustards, use plain Dijon or mix it with fresh (not dried) tarragon or herbes de Provence.

1 tablespoon olive oil

Four 5- to 6-ounce boneless, skinless chicken breast halves, pounded (by the butcher if possible) to half their original thickness

1½ teaspoon salt plus additional for seasoning

Freshly ground pepper

½ cup tarragon- or herbes de Provence—flavored Dijon mustard (or plain Dijon mustard mixed with either 1 table-spoon fresh chopped tarragon or 1 teaspoon herbes de Provence)

2 shallots

4 sprigs parsley, preferably flat-leaf

½ cup dry white wine

1 cup fat-free, reduced-sodium chicken stock

One 8-ounce package of medium egg noodles or egg fettuccine

01 Run the hot-water tap and put 1½ quarts hot tap water in each of 2 pots (one large enough to eventually hold all the water and noodles). Cover and bring both pots to a boil over high heat, 7 to 9 minutes.

02 Meanwhile, put the olive oil in a 12-inch, nonstick sauté pan over medium heat. Season the chicken with salt and pepper. (If the butcher hasn't done so, pound the chicken between two sheets of aluminum foil or wax paper with the side of a cleaver or a meat pounder before seasoning.) Brush one side of each breast with 2 teaspoons of mustard and put the mustard-coated side down in the sauté pan. Brush the top side of the breasts with 2 more teaspoons of mustard. Increase the heat to medium-high. Cook the chicken for 3 minutes.

03 Meanwhile, peel and chop the shallots. Chop the parsley leaves. Turn the chicken over. Add the shallots to the pan, and shake to evenly distribute. Cook for 1 minute. Add the wine and stock. Cover and bring to a boil over high heat.

04 When the water for the noodles boils, transfer the water from the smaller pot to the larger pot. Add the 1½ tea-spoons of salt to the larger pot and add the noodles. Stir well and cook for 5 minutes, or until the noodles are firm but tender. Drain.

05 Meanwhile, uncover the pan with the chicken breasts and let liquid reduce over high heat. As soon as the chicken shows no pink inside (cut into one piece to check if you're not sure), remove the chicken to a plate and cover with foil to keep warm. Add the remaining mustard to the pan. Stir with a wooden spoon just until the mixture begins to thicken, about 1 minute. Add the drained noodles to the pan and toss briefly.

06 With a slotted spoon or tongs, scoop out the noodles and put them on a large platter. Put the chicken on top of the noodles. Using a rubber scraper, pour any sauce left in the pan on top of the chicken. Sprinkle with the parsley.

Chicken Cacciatore

SERVES: 4
CALORIES: 454.17

FAT: 5.69g /11.70%
SATURATED FAT: 1.20g

Though recipes labeled *alla cacciatora* (hunter's style) in Italy don't necessarily have to have chicken or tomatoes, Americans expect both in their chicken cacciatore. Chianti or Barbera are perfect for this dish because both wines have high acidity, which holds up to the acid in the tomatoes. That's why we drink so much Chianti with spaghetti and tomato sauce! If you can't find fresh tarragon, double the parsley rather than using dried tarragon.

Olive oil cooking spray

6 skinless chicken thighs (about 1½ pounds)

1 teaspoon salt plus additional for seasoning

Freshly ground pepper

2 cloves garlic

1 medium onion (about 8 ounces)

6 ounces button mushrooms

½ cup Chianti, Barbera, or similar red wine
with good acidity

One 14.5-ounce can crushed tomatoes

3 or 4 sprigs fresh tarragon, enough for 1 tablespoon of chopped leaves

2 sprigs parsley, preferably flat-leaf,
enough for 1 tablespoon of chopped leaves

1 cup instant polenta

01 Spray a 12-inch, nonstick sauté pan with olive oil spray and put over medium heat. With a cleaver, cut the thighs in half crosswise by whacking through the middle of the bone in each. Season the chicken with salt and pepper. Raise the heat under the pan to high and add the chicken. Brown on one side for 3 minutes.

02 Meanwhile, peel the garlic. Quarter and peel the onion. Put both in a food processor and pulse until chopped. (Or chop by hand.) Slice the mushrooms. Turn the chicken over and add the garlic, onion, and mushrooms to the pan. Cook for 2 minutes, stirring or shaking the pan to evenly distribute the vegetables.

03 Meanwhile, run the hot-water tap. Put the 1 teaspoon salt and 3½ cups hot tap water in a large, heavy saucepan. Cover and bring to a boil over high heat, about 3 minutes. Add the wine to the chicken. Open the can of tomatoes and add the tomatoes and juice to the chicken. Mix well, cover, and bring to a boil. Meanwhile, chop the tarragon leaves and parsley leaves.

04 When the chicken mixture has come to a boil, reduce the heat to a brisk simmer. Add the tarragon, half of the parsley, and salt and pepper to taste. Stir to mix. Cook until the chicken shows no pink inside. (Cut into one piece to check if you're not sure.)

05 Meanwhile, when the water in the saucepan comes to a boil, gradually pour in the polenta while stirring constantly with a sturdy whisk. When the polenta comes to a boil, lower the heat to medium and stir for about 2 minutes, or until the polenta thickens and loses its grainy taste and texture. Pour the polenta onto a platter and spread it out evenly with a large, rubber spatula. Put the chicken on the polenta and pour the sauce over. Sprinkle the remaining parsley on top.

Turkey Tacos with Red Pepper Salsa

SERVES:	4	FAT:	3.41g /5.42%
CALORIES:	578.26	SATURATED FAT:	.43g

This is a fun dish for kids. But when they tell you how good it tastes, don't mention how good it is for them. (Look at those fat numbers, Mom.) Make sure you have plenty of napkins. Tacos are messy.

Canola oil spray
1½ to 2 pounds turkey cutlets
2½ teaspoons ground cumin
¼ to ½ teaspoon ground chipotle or
   cayenne pepper
Salt
⅓ cup dry white wine or fat-free, reduced-sodium
   chicken stock
1 bunch watercress
One 7-ounce jar roasted red bell peppers
4 ounces sweet onion, such as Vidalia
½ cup fresh cilantro leaves, well packed
½ lime
Twelve 6-inch, low-fat flour tortillas
1 cup nonfat sour cream or nonfat plain yogurt

01 Spray a 12-inch, nonstick skillet with canola oil spray and put over medium heat. Cut the turkey cutlets crosswise into strips about ½ inch wide. Add to the pan and increase the heat to high. Season with the cumin, chipotle pepper, and salt to taste. Stir for 2 minutes, then add the wine. Cook, stirring periodically until almost all the liquid evaporates, about 3 minutes. Remove from the heat.

02 Meanwhile, cut ½ inch from the bottom of the watercress bunch. Put the watercress in a salad spinner and fill with water. Drain and spin dry. Wrap in paper towels to remove excess moisture. Put into a serving bowl or on a plate.

03 Drain the roasted peppers in a small colander. Meanwhile, peel and quarter the onion. Put the roasted peppers, onion, and cilantro leaves in a food processor. Pulse until coarsely chopped. Juice the lime half and add to the food processor with salt to taste. Pulse until well combined but still slightly chunky. Put into a serving bowl.

04 Spread the tortillas on a microwave-safe plate and cover with a paper towel. Cook in a microwave oven on high power for 30 seconds. Meanwhile, spoon the cooked turkey onto a platter. Put the sour cream in a small serving bowl. To assemble a taco, lay a tortilla flat and put a few sprigs of the watercress down the center. Then add 1 to 2 ounces of turkey (about ⅓ cup), 1 tablespoon of sour cream, and 1 tablespoon of salsa. Do not overfill. Fold and eat. Serve 3 tacos per person.

Turkey Burgers with Carrot-Dill Coleslaw

SERVES: 4

CALORIES: 378.64

FAT: 10.04g /24.57%

SATURATED FAT: 2.09g

At a luncheon I attended at the famed "21" restaurant in New York, someone asked the chef about the seasonings in the restaurant's signature hamburger. He begged off specifics but did say it was essentially a cooked steak tartare. I've put steak tartare seasonings in this much leaner turkey burger, which is kept moist with egg substitute. You can save a few grams of fat by using English muffins instead of sesame seed hamburger buns, but the muffins aren't quite as moist.

Olive oil spray

1 large shallot

2 tablespoons drained capers

4 sprigs parsley, preferably flat-leaf

2 tablespoons Worcestershire sauce

1 tablespoon Dijon mustard

¼ cup egg substitute

Salt

Freshly ground pepper

1 pound ground turkey breast meat

4 sesame seed hamburger buns

12 ounces green or red cabbage

2 medium carrots

8 to 10 large sprigs fresh dill, enough for ¼ cup
   of chopped leaves

⅓ cup light mayonnaise

2 tablespoons cider vinegar

1 teaspoon sugar

1 medium to large tomato (optional)

Ketchup (optional)

01 Spray a heavy, 12-inch, nonstick skillet with olive oil spray and put over medium-low heat. Peel and halve the shallot. With the motor of a food processor running, drop the shallot down the chute. Scrape down the sides of the bowl with a rubber spatula and add the capers, parsley leaves, Worcestershire sauce, mustard, egg substitute, and salt and pepper to taste. Turn on the machine to mix well while you put the turkey in a mixing bowl.

02 Add the contents of the food processor to the turkey and mix well. Form into a flattened ball. Score into 4 equal sections and form into 4 patties, each 3 to 3½ inches in diameter. Put the turkey into the skillet and raise the heat to medium. Cover and cook for 4 minutes. Quickly wash your hands and the food processor with soapy water and rinse.

03 While the turkey cooks, toast the hamburger buns in a toaster oven.

04 Meanwhile, remove the core from the cabbage and shred using the shredding attachment of the food processor or the large holes of a four-sided grater. Put the cabbage in a large mixing bowl. Turn the burgers over and cook on the other side for 4 minutes or until no pink remains in the center. Peel and shred the carrots in the food processor or with the four-sided grater. Add to the cabbage. Chop the dill leaves and add to the cabbage and carrots.

05 In a small bowl, mix together the mayonnaise, vinegar, sugar, and salt and pepper to taste. Add to the cabbage and carrots and mix thoroughly. If using a tomato, cut it into 4 slices. Serve the turkey burgers on the toasted hamburger buns with a slice of tomato, if desired, and coleslaw on the side. Serve the ketchup at the table, if desired.

Spaghetti Squash with Turkey Bolognese Sauce

SERVES:	4	FAT:	9.11g /24.75%
CALORIES:	330.18	SATURATED FAT:	3.0g

While reading a turkey chili recipe a lightbulb went off in my brain. If turkey can be substituted for beef and pork in chili, why not in a meaty pasta sauce? This sauce also proves that a small amount of fat—in this case heavy cream—can be added for flavor and mouthfeel without sending the total fat content over the limit.

One 2½- to 3-pound spaghetti squash
Olive oil spray
3 ounces turkey bacon
12 ounces ground turkey breast meat
1 small onion (about 4 ounces)
1 rib celery
Two 15-ounce cans tomato sauce
⅓ cup dry white wine
2 tablespoons heavy cream
½ teaspoon ground nutmeg, preferably
   freshly grated
Salt
Freshly ground pepper
Grated Parmesan cheese to pass at the table

01 Cut the squash in half, lengthwise, and scoop out the seeds. Wrap the cut sides of each half tightly with plastic wrap. Put, cut side up, in a microwave oven on high for 13 minutes, or until the strands become loose and tender when scooped with a spoon.

02 Meanwhile, spray a 12-inch, nonstick sauté pan with olive oil spray and put over medium-high heat. Coarsely chop the bacon. Add the bacon and ground turkey to the pan. Cook, breaking up any large clumps of meat with a wooden spoon.

03 While the meat cooks, peel and quarter the onion. Trim the celery and cut into 4 crosswise pieces. Put the onion and celery in a food processor and pulse several times until just chopped. (Or chop by hand.) Add the vegetables to the skillet, increase the heat to high, and cook for 2 minutes, stirring once or twice. Meanwhile open the cans of tomato sauce. Add the tomato sauce and wine to the skillet. Cover and bring to a boil, stirring once or twice.

04 Uncover the pan and add the cream, nutmeg, and salt and pepper to taste. Reduce the heat and simmer gently until the squash is ready. Do not boil.

05 When the squash is done, scoop out the strands into a bowl with a large metal spoon. Season with salt and fluff with a large fork. Put on a serving platter or individual plates. Top with the sauce. Pass the cheese at the table.

Asian Duck Salad

SERVES: 4
CALORIES: 238.76

FAT: 5.57g /20.72%
SATURATED FAT: .74g

Duck is particularly versatile for sautéed dishes, stir-fries, and warm salads like this one. Because duck breast is meatier than chicken or turkey, a 4- to 5-ounce portion (raw) is plenty. The concern about undercooked poultry doesn't apply to duck, especially duck breasts, which start to toughen if cooked more than medium-rare. The 2-minute resting period also helps to tenderize the meat by letting the fibers relax after cooking.

Canola oil spray
2 boneless duck breast halves, about 2 pounds
   with the skin on
Salt
Freshly ground black pepper
1 bunch watercress
1 pound Chinese cabbage, napa cabbage,
   or romaine lettuce
2 medium carrots (6 to 8 ounces total)
One 2-inch piece of fresh ginger
2 limes
1 tablespoon Asian sesame oil
2 tablespoons fish sauce or soy sauce
2 tablespoons rice wine vinegar
¼ to ½ teaspoon cayenne pepper or red
   pepper flakes

01   Spray a cast-iron or other heavy skillet with the cooking spray and put it over medium heat. Remove the skin from the duck breasts by loosening it at one end with a sharp paring knife, then pulling it back, using the tip of the knife to help you along. Season the breasts with salt and black pepper. Add the duck to the skillet, cover, and cook for 5 minutes on one side.

02   Meanwhile, cut off and discard the bottom 1 inch from the watercress stems. Cut the remainder in half and put in a salad spinner. Cut off the bottom 1 inch from the cabbage and discard any damaged leaves. Cut the cabbage crosswise into ½-inch-wide strips. Put in the salad spinner. Fill with cold water, drain, and spin dry. Blot with paper towels to remove excess moisture.

03   Peel and shred the carrots using the large holes of a four-sided grater or the shredding attachment of a food processor. Put the carrots, watercress, and cabbage into a large mixing bowl.

04   Turn the duck over, increase the heat to medium-high, and cook for 3 minutes. Meanwhile, peel and halve the ginger. Using the steel chopping blade, turn on the motor of a food processor and drop the ginger down the chute. While the ginger is being chopped, juice the limes. Turn off the food processor and scrape down the sides of the bowl with a rubber spatula. Add the lime juice, sesame oil, fish sauce, vinegar, hot pepper, and salt to taste. Process the dressing for 15 seconds.

05   When the duck is done, remove it from the skillet and wrap it in aluminum foil. Set aside for 2 minutes. Toss the salad with all the dressing. Cut the duck into thin slices on the diagonal. Add to the salad and toss again. Divide among 4 plates.

Seafood

Seafood is a triple threat when it comes to low-fat, fifteen-minute meals: It's lean, cooks quickly, and offers great variety.

Naturally, with so many fish in the sea, some have more fat than others. Pollock, grouper, cod, mahi mahi, snapper, whiting, monkfish, rainbow trout, and yellowfin tuna all have less than .5 grams of fat per ounce. Swordfish, shark, lake trout, and catfish have a little more than 1 gram of fat per ounce. Salmon and mackerel have quite a bit more. But some of these fattier fish—notably salmon, mackerel, and lake trout—are high in heart healthy Omega 3 fatty acids. Yellowfin tuna has the best of both worlds, low fat but high Omega 3. Striped bass (with .7 grams of fat per ounce), rainbow trout, shark, and swordfish have moderate amounts of Omega 3.

So don't get into a tizzy if your fat allotment goes a tad overboard by eating the Honey-Mustard Salmon with Cucumber-Dill Salad (page 63), which is the only dish in the book that exceeds the 12 grams of fat, 30 percent fat guideline. In fact, be wary of voodoo nutritional analysis when it comes to salmon. Farm-raised Atlantic salmon, which is used in this dish and is by far the most widely available type, has just over 3 grams of fat per ounce. But some recipes show a fat content that reflects wild Pacific salmon at 1.8 grams per ounce, though they don't say so. Wild salmon, available primarily in late spring and summer, is a very small portion of overall salmon consumption.

Because freshness and quality are so important with seafood, buy whatever looks best, regardless of what the recipe dictates. For this reason, and because the selection of seafood isn't the same across the country, I've listed alternatives when possible. For example, in Snapper Veracruz (page 59), sea bass, pollock, haddock, cod, rockfish—any firm, white-fleshed fish, really—can be used. Mussels can be substituted for clams in Clams and Asparagus with Black Bean Sauce (page 66). The shrimp in Shrimp with Mango Salsa (page 68) could trade places with the scallops in Pan-Seared Scallops with Napa Cabbage and Gingered Carrots (page 70). The tuna in Tuna Steak au Poivre with Buttermilk Mashed Potatoes (page 60) could become a salmon steak with Pinot Noir used in the sauce instead of Shiraz or Zinfandel.

Frozen fish is often a perfectly acceptable alternative to fresh fish. It may even be superior if the fish was flash frozen just after being caught and kept at the proper temperature (well below zero). "Fresh" fish can be several days or more old by the time you purchase it. Properly frozen fish should be tightly wrapped, rock hard, and glossy with even color and no white spots that indicate freezer burn. Often, and in the case of shrimp virtually always, frozen seafood is defrosted and sold that way.

Fillets are the most convenient cut of fish because they have no bones, except occasional small pin bones, which can be removed with needle-nose pliers or strong tweezers. Steaks with many bones, like salmon steaks, hold up better on the grill, however. Other steaks, such as swordfish and tuna, have no bones but get their name from their meaty appearance. Make sure fillets have a bright clear look with uniform color and no gaps in the flesh. All seafood should have a clean sea-breeze scent. With the exception of Clams and Asparagus with Black Bean Sauce (page 66), recipes in this chapter allow five to six ounces of seafood, or more, per person.

Fish is done when it springs back after being pressed with a finger. If the fish flakes when pressed, it's overdone. If the finger leaves an indentation, or the flesh is a bit squishy, the fish is underdone. The exceptions are meaty fish like the tuna in Tuna Steak au Poivre with Buttermilk Mashed Potatoes (page 60), which is cooked the way I would cook a beef steak, rare to medium-rare. However, unlike beef, fish cooked do this degree will be cool in the center.

All shellfish cook quickly, but shelled shrimp, scallops, shucked oysters, and crab meat (especially jumbo lump crab meat with virtually no shells) are particularly convenient because unlike mussels and clams, they don't require cleaning. But even that is changing as some companies offer cleaned frozen mussels and clams. (See page 149.)

Shelled shrimp, used in Shrimp with Mango Salsa (page 68) and in recipes elsewhere in the book, normally come in only one or two sizes. If you have a choice, get the size as close as possible to 21 to 24 count per pound, which is the size I used in all the recipes in the book. I don't devein shrimp, so add a few minutes to the preparation if you want to perform that task. While raw, frozen, shelled shrimp are convenient, I'd steer clear of cooked shrimp (frozen or not) unless they are destined for cold dishes. Reheating is bound to make them rubbery.

Sea scallops are available year-round, and the smaller, more expensive bay scallops only in winter. But sea scallops have more flavor anyway. Sea scallops come with a small strip attached to one side of the muscle, which I remove before cooking. Cleaned squid is now widely available and inexpensive.

As with most other dishes in this book, pan-frying, sautéing, poaching, or steaming on top of the stove are the preferred methods for cooking seafood. You can also put fish on a gas grill or under a broiler, if they heat up quickly. While waiting for that to happen, fish can marinate in a mixture of olive oil, lemon juice, and garlic, or one of sesame oil, soy sauce, and rice wine. A microwave oven is faster than the stove top, broiler, or grill, but doesn't give you the same flavor.

Snapper Veracruz

A mainstay in many Mexican restaurants, *pescado a la Veracruzana* (fish Veracruz-style) is named for the Mexican coastal town founded by Cortez in 1519. While snapper is the preferred fish, you can use the flavorful sauce with a variety of white-fleshed fish like sea bass, rockfish, and pollock, as well as with pork and chicken. If you want a spicier sauce, use more pickled jalapeño or a larger fresh jalapeño, or keep the seeds and membranes of the fresh pepper because that's where most of the heat resides.

1 cup basmati rice

1 teaspoon salt plus additional for seasoning

Olive oil spray

2 cloves garlic

1 tablespoon sliced pickled jalapeño peppers
    or 1 fresh jalapeño pepper

1 small onion (about 4 ounces)

1 large tomato (about 12 ounces)

⅓ cup fresh cilantro leaves

⅓ cup pimiento-stuffed olives (about 8 medium)

Freshly ground pepper

Four 6-ounce red snapper, sea bass, pollock,
    haddock, cod, or rockfish fillets, pin bones
    removed

1 teaspoon chili powder

01 While the hot-water tap runs, put the rice in a 2-quart saucepan. Add 2 cups hot tap water and the 1 teaspoon salt. Cover and bring to a boil over high heat. Reduce the heat to low and cook for 10 minutes. Turn the heat off and keep covered until ready to serve. (Or put the rice, 2 cups of hot tap water, and the 1 teaspoon salt in a 2-quart, microwave-safe container. Cover and cook in a microwave oven on high power for 10 minutes. Keep covered until ready to serve.)

02 Meanwhile, spray a heavy saucepan (preferably nonstick) with olive oil spray and put it over medium heat. Peel the garlic. With the motor of a food processor running, drop the garlic and jalapeño down the chute and finely chop. (If using a fresh jalapeño, stem and seed it first.) Stop the motor and scrape down the sides of the bowl with a rubber spatula. Peel and quarter the onion. Add to the processor and pulse a few times to chop very coarsely. Add the mixture to the saucepan.

03 Core and quarter the tomato. Add the tomato, cilantro, olives, and salt and black pepper to taste to the processor. Pulse until the mixture is fully combined but still chunky. Add to the saucepan, cover, and bring to a boil. Reduce the heat to a simmer and stir the sauce once or twice.

04 Meanwhile, spray a heavy, 12-inch, nonstick skillet with olive oil spray and put it over medium heat. Season the fleshy side of the fish with the chili powder, salt, and black pepper. Add the fish to the skillet, skin side down. Increase the heat to medium-high and cook for 2 minutes.

05 Pour the tomato sauce over the fish, cover, and cook for 6 minutes, or until the fish feels springy to the touch. When sauce reaches a boil, lower the heat to a simmer. Divide the fish, sauce, and rice among 4 plates.

Tuna Steak au Poivre with Buttermilk Mashed Potatoes

SERVES: 4	**FAT:** 8.08ɢ /21.48%
CALORIES: 346.77	**SATURATED FAT:** 2.17ɢ

Steak and mashed potatoes may not seem like a low-fat meal, but they are when the steak is tuna, and the potatoes don't have butter and cream. Tuna can handle the same big red wines that beef does, as long as the wine is low in tannin, that astringent stuff that makes your mouth pucker like strong tea. An Australian Shiraz might be the best match because its often peppery edge will complement the peppercorn crust of the tuna. A California Zinfandel would be my second choice.

2 large red-skinned potatoes (about 1 pound total)

1 teaspoon salt plus additional for seasoning

4 teaspoons peppercorns

Two 12-ounce tuna steaks, each about 1-inch thick

¾ cup buttermilk

10 chives, enough for about 1½ tablespoons when chopped

¾ cup dry red wine with low tannins, such as an Australian
 Shiraz or California Zinfandel

2 tablespoons oyster sauce

Freshly ground pepper to taste

01 Put a cast-iron or other heavy skillet over medium heat. Quarter the potatoes lengthwise. (Do not peel.) Cut the pieces crosswise into thin slices. While the hot-water tap runs, put the potatoes in a large saucepan or deep skillet. Barely cover with hot tap water and put over high heat. Add the 1 teaspoon salt. Cover and cook for 12 minutes or until the potatoes are just tender. (Or put the potatoes, ¼ cup hot tap water, and the 1 teaspoon salt in a 2-quart, microwave-safe container. Cover and put in a microwave oven on high power for 10 minutes.)

02 Put the peppercorns in a Ziploc plastic bag and crush them with a rolling pin or bottle. (Or grind them on the coarse setting of a pepper mill, which will take a bit longer.) Season the tuna steaks with salt and press both sides into the crushed peppercorns.

03 Increase the heat under the skillet to high and put the tuna inside. Cook for 1½ minutes. Turn the steaks over and cook for another 1½ minutes. While the tuna cooks, warm the milk in a small saucepan over medium heat. (Or put the buttermilk in a covered, microwave-safe container and heat in a microwave oven on high power for 1 minute.) Chop the chives.

04 Remove the steaks from the skillet and put them on a cutting board. Add the wine and oyster sauce to the skillet and put over high heat. Stir periodically with a wooden spoon until the sauce just begins to thicken—about 2 minutes. Meanwhile, cut the steaks into ½-inch-thick slices—they will be rare in the middle—and place them on a platter. Cover with aluminum foil to keep warm.

05 Drain the cooked potatoes and put them in a food processor with ½ cup of the buttermilk, the chives, and salt and pepper to taste. Pulse just until well combined. Leave a bit lumpy if desired or pulse until smooth. Don't overprocess. Add as much of the remaining ¼ cup of milk as desired to achieve the texture you want. (Or use a hand potato masher and whip the milk at the end with a large fork or wooden spoon.) Pour the sauce over the tuna and serve with the potatoes.

Honey-Mustard Salmon with Cucumber-Dill Salad

SERVES: 4	FAT: 17.48g /40.47%
CALORIES: 401.24	SATURATED FAT: 3.27g

This is the only recipe in the book in which the grams of fat and percentage of fat are over the limit. But there's nothing unhealthful in this dish. Salmon is naturally fatty, but the fat is heart-healthy Omega 3 fatty acids. I could have reduced the fat in this dish by making the portion of salmon smaller, and I could have lowered the percentage of fat by adding more vegetables. But that just seemed silly. The dish is terrific—and healthful—the way it is.

Canola oil spray
**Four 5-ounce salmon fillets with
   pin bones removed**
Salt
Freshly ground pepper
2 cups nonfat plain yogurt
**1½ pounds English (seedless) cucumbers
   or other cucumbers**
4 ounces sweet onion, such as Vidalia
**8 to 10 large sprigs fresh dill, enough for
   ¼ cup leaves chopped**
**4 tablespoons honey mustard or sweet
   and hot mustard**
1 tablespoon cider vinegar

01 Turn on the broiler and set the broiler rack 6 inches from the heat source. Spray a large, cast-iron skillet with canola oil spray, and put it over high heat on top of the stove. Season the salmon with salt and pepper to taste. Put the salmon skin side down in the skillet. Cover and cook for 5 minutes.

02 Meanwhile, put the yogurt in a fine mesh strainer over a bowl to drain excess liquid. Peel the cucumbers and halve lengthwise. (Scoop out the seeds if using regular cucumbers.) Thinly slice crosswise. Put the cucumber in a tea towel and squeeze out some of the moisture. Put the cucumbers into a large mixing bowl. Peel and thinly slice the onion. Add to the mixing bowl. Chop the leaves from the dill. Add to the mixing bowl.

03 Brush each salmon fillet with 1 tablespoon of the mustard and put under the broiler for 2 minutes. Remove the skillet from the broiler. Spoon the pan juices over the salmon and cover to keep warm.

04 In a small bowl, mix the drained yogurt, vinegar, and salt and pepper to taste. Add to the cucumber mixture. Toss well. Serve with the salmon.

Salmon Galette with Eggs

The French are fond of making galettes from potatoes. This galette is a seafood version of corned-beef hash. It's leaner, of course. Sounds classier than corned-beef hash, too. Most canned salmon contains skin and bones. Look for canned salmon labeled "boneless and skinless pink salmon," which is not only more convenient but has less fat than canned salmon labeled "Alaska salmon." This dish is also a good way to use up that leftover poached salmon from Saturday dinner.

2 large potatoes (about 1 pound) or 1-pound bag of frozen (uncooked) hash brown potatoes

Canola oil spray

Two 6-ounce cans boneless and skinless pink salmon

1 bunch green onions (scallions)

6 to 8 large sprigs dill, enough for 3 tablespoons chopped leaves

Salt

Freshly ground pepper

4 English muffins

4 large eggs

Paprika

01 Using the shredding attachment of a food processor or the largest holes of a four-sided grater, grate the potatoes. (Don't peel.) Put them in a tea towel and squeeze out as much moisture as possible with one good wring. Put the potatoes in a mixing bowl. (If using frozen hash browns, empty the bag into a colander. Rinse briefly under warm running water to break up any clumps. Then wring in a tea towel.) Spray a 12-inch, nonstick skillet with canola oil spray and put over medium heat.

02 Open and drain the cans of salmon and add to the potatoes, flaking the fish with a fork. Trim the bulb ends of the green onions and cut them crosswise into thirds. Set aside the top third (the dark green part) and put the rest in the food processor with the chopping blade. Add the leaves from the dill and pulse until chopped. (Or chop by hand.) Add to the mixing bowl. Season with salt and pepper to taste and mix well.

03 Increase the heat under the skillet to medium-high. Add the salmon and potato mixture to the skillet and press with a wide spatula or wooden spoon to make a firm pancake. Cook for 5 minutes.

04 Meanwhile, split the English muffins and toast them to the desired degree of doneness in a toaster or toaster oven. When the galette has cooked for 5 minutes on one side, slide it onto a large plate and cover with another plate the same size. Turn it over and, guiding it with a spatula, slide it back into the skillet, uncooked side down.

05 Make 4 indentations into the galette with the bottom of a ladle or large spoon. Break one egg into a small bowl and slide it into one of the indentations. Repeat with the remaining eggs. Cover and cook for 3 minutes, or until the yolks are set and the whites opaque.

06 Meanwhile, mince the reserved tops from the green onions. When the eggs are cooked, sprinkle with the paprika and minced green onion tops. Bring the galette in the pan to the table and cut into 4 wedges with the front edge of the spatula. Use the spatula to place the wedges on individual plates. Serve with the English muffins.

Clams and Asparagus with Black Bean Sauce

SERVES: 4
CALORIES: 309.66

FAT: 2.83g / 7.81%
SATURATED FAT: .16g

Clams and black bean sauce have always been a well-known Chinese combination. Instead of the more traditional salted and fermented black soybeans, I use bottled black bean sauce, which is more widely available and simplifies preparation. I also use low-sodium chicken stock and half the normal amount of salt for cooking the rice. Otherwise the dish is too salty. In place of clams, you can try mussels, shrimp, or scallops.

1 cup basmati rice

½ teaspoon salt

1½ cups fat-free, reduced-sodium chicken stock

3 dozen littleneck clams

1 pound asparagus (thin to medium thickness)

3 cloves garlic

One 2-inch piece fresh ginger

2 tablespoons bottled black bean sauce

2 teaspoons cornstarch

2 green onions (scallions)

01 While the hot-water tap runs, put the rice in a 2-quart saucepan. Add 2 cups hot tap water and the salt. Cover and bring to a boil over high heat. Reduce the heat to low and cook for 10 minutes or until all the water is absorbed. Turn the heat off and keep covered until ready to serve. (Or put the rice, 2 cups hot tap water, and the salt in a 2-quart, microwave-safe container. Cover and put in a microwave oven on high power for 10 minutes. Keep covered until ready to serve.)

02 Meanwhile, put 1 cup of the stock in a wok, 12-inch sauté pan, or Dutch oven over medium-high heat and cover. Put the clams in a bowl under cool running water and quickly scrub them with a vegetable brush, putting them in a colander once scrubbed. (This should take about 3 minutes.) Add the clams to the pan. Cover and increase the heat to high. As the clams open over the next several minutes, remove them to a shallow serving bowl with a slotted spoon or skimmer. Cover to keep warm. (Discard any clams that don't open.)

03 Meanwhile, cut off the bottom inch from the asparagus. Cut rest of the asparagus on the diagonal into 1½-inch pieces. Peel the garlic. Peel and halve the ginger. With the motor of a food processor running, drop the garlic and ginger down the chute. Turn off the machine when the garlic and ginger are completely chopped. Scrape down the sides of the bowl with a rubber spatula.

04 Add the black bean sauce and cornstarch to the food processor bowl along with the remaining stock. Pulse a few times to mix well. As soon as the clams have been removed from the pan, add the asparagus to the pan and cover. Cook for 1 minute. Add the black bean sauce mixture and mix well. Return the clams to the pan and cover. If using a sauté pan, shake the pan a few times to make sure the clams are well coated. Stir the ingredients if using a wok or Dutch oven.

05 Trim and finely chop the green onions, including the green tops. Remove the lid from the pan. When the sauce has begun to thicken, remove the clams to the shallow serving bowl. Pour the sauce and asparagus over. Sprinkle the green onions on top and serve with the rice.

Shrimp with Mango Salsa

SERVES: 4
CALORIES: 433.42

FAT: 6.48g /13.97%
SATURATED FAT: .89g

This recipe is inspired by a dish that was part of the cooking competition at the Gilroy Garlic Festival when I was master of ceremonies a number of years ago. As much as I like the garlic and shrimp flavors, I like the hot jalapeño mingled with the sweet mango even more. A little tequila gives it some south-of-the-border sass.

1 cup basmati rice

1 teaspoon salt plus additional for seasoning

2 tablespoons sliced pickled jalapeño peppers from a jar or 2 whole fresh jalapeños, or to taste

4 ounces sweet onion such as Vidalia, or mild red onion

1 small red bell pepper

½ cup well-packed fresh cilantro leaves

2 ripe medium-size ripe but firm mangoes

2 limes

1 tablespoon olive oil

1 pound peeled shrimp, preferably 21 to 24 per pound

2 cloves garlic

¼ cup tequila

01 While the hot-water tap runs, put the rice in a 2-quart saucepan. Add 2 cups hot tap water and the 1 teaspoon salt. Cover and bring to a boil over high heat. Reduce the heat to low and cook for 10 minutes. Turn the heat off and keep covered until ready to serve. (Or put the rice, 2 cups hot tap water, and the 1 teaspoon salt in a 2-quart, microwave-safe container. Cover and microwave on high power for 10 minutes. Keep covered until ready to serve.)

02 With the motor of a food processor running, drop the jalapeño down the chute and finely chop. (If using a fresh jalapeño, stem and seed it first.) Stop the motor and scrape down sides of the bowl with a rubber spatula. Peel and quarter the onion. Cut the top from the bell pepper. Stand it upright and cut down inside the four walls, separating them from the center core and seeds. Put the bell pepper, onion, and all but 1 tablespoon of the cilantro leaves into the food processor. Pulse until chopped but still quite chunky.

03 Place one mango, narrow side down, on a cutting surface. Slice through the mango as close to the pit as possible on one side. (The oval pit in the center of the mango is about ¾-inch wide. Do not peel the mango.) Repeat on the other side. With a teaspoon, scraping as close to the skin as possible, scoop out the flesh in one big piece from each of the two slices. Cut each piece into 4 chunks. Repeat with the second mango.

04 Juice one of the limes. Add the mango, lime juice, and a pinch of salt to the processor and pulse just until the salsa is fully combined but still chunky. Put into a large shallow serving bowl (large enough to hold the mango salsa and the shrimp).

05 Put the oil in a 12-inch, nonstick skillet over medium heat. Season the shrimp with salt. Add to the pan, and raise the heat to medium-high. Peel and chop the garlic. Add the garlic to the pan, turn the shrimp over, and cook for 1 minute.

06 Juice the other lime and combine with the tequila in a small bowl. Add the tequila-lime juice mixture to the pan and cook for 2 minutes. Meanwhile, chop the remaining cilantro leaves. Remove the pan from the heat and fold the shrimp into the salsa. Adjust seasoning, if necessary. Serve with the rice. Sprinkle the remaining cilantro on top of the rice and shrimp.

Pan-Seared Scallops with Napa Cabbage and Gingered Carrots

SERVES: 4	FAT: 7.93g /25.50%
CALORIES: 279.74	SATURATED FAT: 2.43g

Ever since my 12-year-old godson David tasted carrots with candied or crystallized ginger, he won't eat them any other way. Who says kids don't like vegetables? Heating the skillet under the broiler, which I learned from Evan Lobel of Lobel's Prime Meats in New York City, is also a great way to cook steaks.

1 pound carrots
1 teaspoon salt plus additional for seasoning
1 tablespoon olive oil
1 pound napa cabbage
Freshly ground pepper
1½ pounds sea scallops
1 teaspoon paprika
1½ tablespoons candied (crystallized) ginger
4 chives
2 tablespoons sherry or raspberry vinegar
1 tablespoon butter

01 Turn on the broiler and set the broiler pan 4 inches from the heat source. Put a cast-iron skillet, large enough to hold all the scallops in one layer without crowding, under the broiler.

02 Peel and trim the carrots and slice by hand or with the slicing attachment of a food processor. Turn on the hot-water tap. Put the carrots and the 1 teaspoon salt in a skillet and add 1 cup hot tap water. Put over medium-high heat and cover.

03 Put the olive oil in a 12-inch sauté pan over medium heat. Cut off the bottom ½ inch from the cabbage and cut the remainder cross-wise into ½-inch-wide strips. You should have 4 to 5 cups. Rinse in a colander briefly, then add to the pan. Season well with salt and pepper. Increase the heat to medium-high and cover.

04 Remove the tough, small strip on the sides of the scallops. Halve the scallops, if large, and put into a medium-size bowl. Add the paprika and salt and pepper to taste. Toss to mix well. Remove the skillet from the broiler and add the scallops in a single layer. Return the skillet to the broiler and cook for 2 minutes. Meanwhile, chop the candied ginger and the chives.

05 Turn the scallops over, return them to broiler and cook for 2 minutes. Then remove and cover to keep warm. Add the vinegar to the cabbage, cover, and shake the pan well. As soon as the carrots are just tender, drain and toss them in a dry skillet with the butter and ginger and more salt, if needed. Put the carrots along one side of an oval or rectangular serving platter. Put the scallops in the middle and sprinkle them with the chives. With a slotted spoon, scoop out the cabbage from the pan and put on the opposite side of the platter.

Monkfish Osso Buco

Osso buco with fish? With their round bone in the center, monkfish steaks always reminded me of veal shanks, which are used in that famous Italian braised dish. So I figured, why not a faster, lighter seafood version? All the elements are here, even the lemon-parsley gremolata for garnish. If you can't find monkfish with the bone, try monkfish fillets, other bone-in fish such as cod, halibut, or Chilean sea bass, or meaty boneless steaks like shark, swordfish, or mahi mahi. Couscous or rice can be used in place of polenta.

1 tablespoon olive oil

4 monkfish steaks with the bone in the center (about 7 ounces each) or similar steaks of cod, halibut, or Chilean sea bass

1 teaspoon salt plus additional for seasoning

Freshly ground pepper

¼ cup all-purpose flour

1 medium onion (about 8 ounces)

2 cloves garlic

1 carrot

1 rib celery

1 lemon

2 sprigs parsley, preferably flat-leaf, enough for 1 tablespoon of leaves when chopped

One 14.5-ounce can diced tomatoes or 1 large tomato, about 12 ounces

½ cup dry white wine

2 tablespoons capers, drained

1 cup instant polenta

01　Put the oil in a 12-inch, nonstick sauté pan over medium heat. Season the monkfish with salt and pepper. Put the flour on a sheet of wax paper or a pie plate and dredge the fish in the flour. Shake off any excess flour. Increase the heat in the pan to medium-high and add the monkfish.

02　While the monkfish cooks, peel and quarter the onion. Peel the garlic. Trim, peel, and cut the carrot crosswise into 4 roughly equal pieces. Trim and cut the celery crosswise into 4 roughly equal pieces. Put the vegetables into a food processor. Pulse just until chopped. (Or chop by hand.) Turn the monkfish over and cook for 3 minutes.

03　Meanwhile, run the hot-water tap. Put the 1 teaspoon salt and 3½ cups hot tap water in a large, heavy saucepan. Cover and bring to a boil over high heat, about 3 minutes. With a lemon zester, zest the lemon rind, then mince. (Or grate with a grater.) You should have about 2 teaspoons. (Save the rest of the lemon for another use.) Mince the parsley leaves. Mix the lemon zest and parsley in a small bowl and set aside.

04　Move the monkfish to one side of the sauté pan, and add the onion, garlic, celery, and carrots. Increase the heat to high and stir the vegetables. Cook for 2 minutes while you open the can of tomatoes (or chop the fresh tomato). Add the wine, tomatoes, capers, and salt and pepper to taste to the pan and stir. Spread the monkfish evenly throughout the pan. Spoon some sauce over the top of the fish to moisten. Cover and cook until the fish feels springy to the touch, about 4 minutes. Shake the pan back and forth a few times while the fish cooks.

05　When the water in the saucepan comes to a boil, gradually pour in the polenta while stirring with a sturdy whisk or wooden spoon. Lower the heat to medium and stir for about 2 minutes, or until the polenta thickens and loses its grainy taste and texture. Divide the polenta among 4 soup plates, spreading it out evenly with a rubber spatula. Put the monkfish on the polenta and spoon the sauce over. Sprinkle the lemon-parsley mixture on top.

Seafood Cassoulet

SERVES:	4		FAT:	8.75g / 21.77%
CALORIES:	366.15		SATURATED FAT:	1.36g

Normally, cassoulet is heavy enough to be used for brick mortar. But this seafood version is so light, you can eat it year round and not feel like taking a nap when you finish. Testers who tried this recipe thought it was classy enough to be served for company.

Olive oil spray

1 medium onion (about 8 ounces)

3 cloves garlic

2 ounces Canadian bacon

1 lemon

4 large sprigs fresh tarragon or 2 sprigs parsley, preferably flat-leaf, enough for 1 tablespoon of chopped leaves

Two 8-ounce bottles clam juice

Two 15-ounce cans small white beans, navy beans, Great Northern beans, or cannellini beans

8 ounces cod, halibut, or Chilean sea bass

8 ounces sea scallops

8 ounces raw, peeled shrimp (about 21 to 24 per pound)

Salt

Freshly ground pepper

4 teaspoons extra-virgin olive oil

01 Spray a 12-inch, nonstick sauté pan with olive oil spray and put over medium heat. Peel and quarter the onion. Peel the garlic. Put the onion and garlic into a food processor. Pulse just until chopped. (Or chop by hand.) Scrape into the sauté pan, raise the heat to medium-high, and stir.

02 Coarsely chop the Canadian bacon, add to the pan, and stir. Juice the lemon. Chop the tarragon. Add the lemon juice, half of the tarragon, and the clam juice to the pan. Stir, cover, and bring to a boil over high heat.

03 Open the cans of beans into a colander. Rinse briefly and add to the pan. Cover and bring to a boil.

04 Cut the cod into 4 pieces of equal size. Halve the scallops if large. Season the fish, shrimp, and scallops with salt and pepper. Add the seafood to the pan. Sprinkle with the remaining tarragon. Cover and bring to a boil. Reduce the heat to medium and cook 4 to 5 minutes or until the fish is springy to the touch. Stir gently once or twice. Divide the beans, seafood, and broth among 4 plates. Drizzle each with 1 teaspoon of olive oil.

Cacciucco

SERVES: 4
CALORIES: 459.80

FAT: 9.97g /20.94%
SATURATED FAT 2.53g

Cacciucco is the signature fish stew of Livorno (Leghorn) on the Tyrrhenian Sea coast of Tuscany. Like many other fish stews, it offers enormous possibilities for eating fish and shellfish with a minimum amount of fat. Almost any kind of seafood would be appropriate except for oily fish like tuna or delicate fish like flounder. You can vary the seasonings as well, changing herbs and spices to suit your taste or whim. If you want some authenticity in your cacciucco, try eel or octopus.

Olive oil spray
1 medium onion (about 8 ounces)
4 cloves garlic
1 carrot
1 rib celery
One 14.5-ounce can crushed or diced tomatoes
Two 8-ounce bottles clam juice
4 large sprigs fresh thyme, enough for 1 tablespoon of
    chopped leaves, or 1 teaspoon dried thyme
⅔ cup dry white wine
¾ teaspoon red pepper flakes, or to taste
3 bay leaves
Salt
Freshly ground black pepper
1½ pounds (preferably two 12-ounce fillets) of striped bass,
    red snapper, haddock, tilefish, or grouper
8 ounces cleaned squid bodies or shelled shrimp
1 small, round loaf (12 ounces or less) of country-style
    or sourdough bread
8 sprigs parsley, preferably flat-leaf, enough for
    2 tablespoons when chopped

01 Turn on the broiler and set the broiler rack 6 inches from the heat source. Spray a 12-inch, nonstick sauté pan with olive oil spray and put over medium heat. Peel and quarter the onion. Peel the garlic. Peel and cut the carrot crosswise into 4 pieces. Cut the celery crosswise into 4 pieces. Put the onion, carrot, celery, and 3 cloves of the garlic into a food processor. Pulse just until chopped. (Or chop by hand.) Scrape into the sauté pan and raise the heat to high. Cook for 2 minutes, stirring once or twice.

02 Meanwhile, open the can of tomatoes and the bottles of clam juice. If using fresh thyme, chop the leaves. Add the wine to the sauté pan and cook for 30 seconds. Add the tomatoes with juices, clam juice, thyme, red pepper flakes, bay leaves, and salt and black pepper to taste. Stir well, cover, and bring to a boil over high heat.

03 Meanwhile, cut fish fillets into approximately 2-ounce pieces. Season the fish with salt and add to the sauté pan. Cover and bring to a boil. Reduce the heat and simmer for 3 minutes.

04 While the fish cooks, cut the squid bodies crosswise into rings about ½ inch wide. Cut tentacles if large. (If using shrimp, keep whole.) Cut 4 slices, ½ to ¾ inch thick, from the loaf of bread. Put the slices on a baking sheet and put under the broiler for 1 to 2 minutes on each side or until lightly toasted. Season the squid or shrimp with salt and add to the sauté pan. Cover and cook until the fish are springy to the touch, squid is just firm, and shrimp are pink and just firm.

05 Meanwhile, chop the parsley leaves. Cut the remaining clove of garlic in half. When the bread has been toasted, spray one side with olive oil spray and rub the crusty edges of each slice with the cut side of the garlic. Put a slice of toast in the bottom of 4 soup plates. Stir the parsley into the stew and taste again for salt and black pepper. Divide the seafood among the soup plates and pour the broth over.

Pasta

When I began writing about quick cooking, I started with pastas. I called my quick pastas "throw togethers" because that's what I did. As soon as I came home from work, I'd put the pasta cooking water on the stove to heat up. Then I'd scour the pantry to see what I could throw together with the cooked pasta.

The same concept holds true for low-fat pasta cooking except that you can't just throw anything in with the pasta. Cheeses and meats should be used judiciously. Oils must be measured, not poured. Still, there's a good-sized arsenal with which to do battle on the fifteen-minute, low-fat pasta front.

Thickeners like cream are out but you can create a more than adequate substitute by mixing cornstarch with stock, the way it is done in Pasta with Three-Mushroom Sauce (page 88). Canned nonfat skim milk is then added to provide a creamy taste. You can also achieve that creaminess with nonfat, low-fat, or part-skim ricotta cheese (or cottage cheese), as is done in Pasta Primavera (page 91). Or use pasta cooking water (in Fettuccine with Pesto, Potatoes, and Tomatoes, page 82, and others), which has flavor as well as some starchiness from the pasta.

Stocks, especially chicken stock, can take the place of oil to cook garlic as in Pasta with Broccoli Raab and Feta Cheese (page 85). I still use oil in the dish but only at the very end of preparation, where its taste will be most noticeable.

Tomatoes are perhaps the best fat fighters for pasta. The Spaghetti all'Amatriciana (page 93) uses a fairly traditional but delicious tomato sauce that relies on top-quality canned San Marzano tomatoes, which are available in many markets. Capellini with Southwestern-style Clam Sauce (page 81) is my tomatoey twist on the more common linguine with clam sauce. Instead of using bacon or clams as in the above two recipes, you could make the same tomato sauce with vegetables like zucchini, broccoli, and mushrooms. Or you can make a lean meat ragu like that in Spaghetti Squash with Turkey Bolognese Sauce (page 53).

I use cheese sparingly and rely primarily on grated Romano or Parmesan because they spread their flavor well. Cheese used in cooking is factored into nutritional calculations. Cheese passed at the table is not.

Pasta dishes call for twelve ounces of uncooked pasta (which becomes about 1½ pounds when cooked), enough to feed four people. I started out with one pound of uncooked pasta but the consensus among my recipe testers was that this was too much. The lone exception is Spaghetti all'Amatriciana (page 93), which uses one pound of pasta with its relatively simple tomato sauce.

The increased availability of fresh pasta has helped quick pasta dishes tremendously. In fact, more and more markets are making their own pasta or having it made for them. I use dried capellini (also known as angel hair or *capelli d'angelo*) because it cooks the fastest among dried pastas. Other dried pastas will take longer. Some brands cook faster than others. So check the box for cooking times. I prefer dried Italian pasta because of its firmness and taste. Fresh pasta, regardless of the shape, cooks as fast as or faster than dried capellini.

Because long, thin capellini pasta can make tossing it with vegetables and sauce difficult, I break the noodles in half before cooking. In addition to making it easier to mix with other ingredients, the pasta cooks faster this way, especially when cooked with vegetables as in Pasta Primavera (page 91). It's also easier to eat. Breaking up pasta may seem sacrilegious to purists, but hey, so are fifteen-minute meals.

Several of my volunteer recipe testers wondered why I heat half the cooking water in each of two pots, then combine them to cook the pasta. One suggested, "Just put the one pot on a little earlier!" The reason is that it is difficult to cook pasta within fifteen minutes unless you use two pots and start with hot tap water (see Low-Fat and Quick-Cooking Tips, page 23). The pot that isn't used for cooking the pasta— the smaller of the two pots—isn't dirtied because all you've done is heat water in it. If you still consider this method inconvenient, by all means, use one pot (and cold tap water, if you like). You just won't be able to make the dish in fifteen minutes, unless you've got a turbo-charged stovetop.

While it isn't essential, having a pasta pot with a built-in colander enables you to drain the pasta right over the pot. The pasta can then be transferred to a nearby mixing bowl, sauté pan, or wok. However, draining pasta into a traditional colander in the sink has an advantage over pots with built-in colanders; the emptied pasta pot becomes a perfect container for mixing the cooked pasta and sauce. It's large, so nothing spills out. And it's hot, so the pasta and sauce remain warm. If you're going to use a sauté pan to mix the pasta and sauce, as is called for in several pasta recipes such as Pasta with Broccoli Raab and Feta Cheese (page 85), make sure the pan is sufficiently large, at least a 4-quart capacity.

Regardless of how you heat the water or what type of pasta you use, two teaspoons of salt should be added to the cooking water for twelve ounces of raw pasta. One recipe tester said that her pasta tasted "rather bland." When I asked if she used the required amount of salt in the cooking water, she said, "I didn't use any salt. We don't salt anything because

of my husband's high blood pressure. Is that important?" Yes, very! Pasta, whether it's going to be used in a low-fat dish or not, needs a generous amount of salt. While the amount of salt I use may seem like a lot, a good deal of it goes down the drain with the cooking water. Obviously, you shouldn't do anything you feel compromises your health. But you should also understand what happens when pasta is undersalted.

Capellini with Southwestern-style Clam Sauce

SERVES:	4	FAT:	7.13g /15.61%
CALORIES:	433.09	SATURATED FAT:	.95g

Spaghetti with jalapeño peppers and cilantro isn't so weird when you consider pizza with ham and pineapple or duck sausage. Weird or not, this dish is delicious. No cheese is called for because Italians don't normally put cheese on pasta with seafood. But since they don't eat cilantro either, go ahead and sprinkle on some cheese if you like.

½ cup dry white wine

One 8-ounce bottle clam juice

5 cloves garlic

2 tablespoons sliced jalapeño peppers from
   a jar or 2 whole fresh jalapeños, or to taste

One 14.5-ounce can whole or diced tomatoes

1 tablespoon tomato paste

Three 6.5-ounce cans chopped clams

½ cup packed fresh cilantro leaves

12 ounces fresh linguine or spaghetti,
   or dried capellini (angel hair)

2 teaspoons salt plus additional for seasoning

1 tablespoon extra-virgin olive oil

01 Run the hot-water tap and put 2 quarts hot tap water in each of 2 pots (one large enough to eventually hold all the water and pasta). Cover and bring both pots to a boil over high heat, 8 to 10 minutes.

02 Meanwhile, put the wine and clam juice in a 12-inch sauté pan over high heat. Peel the garlic. With the motor of a food processor running, drop the garlic and the jalapeño down the chute and finely chop. Turn off the motor and scrape down the sides of the bowl with a rubber spatula. Add the tomatoes with juices and the tomato paste. Pulse until well combined but not totally pureed.

03 Scrape the tomato mixture into the sauté pan and cook for 4 minutes while you open the cans of clams and chop the cilantro. Add the clams with juices to the pan. Cook for 3 minutes, then turn off the heat.

04 When the water boils, transfer the water from the smaller pot into the larger pot. Cut (if fresh) or break (if dried) the pasta in half. Add the 2 teaspoons salt and the pasta to the pot. Stir, cover, and return to a boil. Stir again, partially cover, and cook for 3 to 4 minutes, stirring at least one more time, or until the pasta is done to your taste.

05 Meanwhile, stir the cilantro into the tomato sauce and add more salt if necessary. When the pasta is cooked, drain, and put into the sauté pan along with the olive oil. Toss well. Divide the pasta among 4 soup plates or pasta bowls and top with the tomato sauce.

Fettuccine with Pesto, Potatoes, and Tomatoes

Though you can make this dish any time of the year, it's especially good in summer when local, more flavorful basil is available. Toasting the pine nuts and adding a little extra garlic makes up for cutting back on the oil in this recipe.

2 large red-skinned potatoes (14 to
   16 ounces total)
2 teaspoons salt plus additional for seasoning
2 tablespoons pine nuts or walnuts
3 cloves garlic
24 small cherry tomatoes
12 ounces fresh fettuccine or dried capellini
   (angel hair)
2 cups well-packed basil leaves
1 tablespoon extra-virgin olive oil
¼ cup grated Parmesan cheese plus additional
   to pass at the table

01 Run the hot-water tap and put 2 quarts hot tap water in each of 2 pots (one large enough to eventually hold all the water, pasta, and potatoes). Cover and bring both pots to a boil over high heat, 8 to 10 minutes. Meanwhile, quarter each potato lengthwise. Then cut crosswise into ¼-inch-thick slices. Add the potatoes and the 2 teaspoons salt to the larger of the two pots. Stir and cover.

02 While the potatoes cook, put the pine nuts in a small skillet over medium heat and toast for 5 minutes. Shake periodically to toast evenly. Lower the heat if necessary to prevent burning. Peel the garlic. With the motor of a food processor running, drop the garlic down the chute. When finely chopped, scrape down the sides of the bowl with a rubber spatula. Halve the cherry tomatoes and set aside in a small bowl.

03 When the water boils in the small pot, pour it into the larger pot with the potatoes. Cover and bring to a boil. Cut (if fresh) or break (if dried) the pasta in half. Add to the pot and stir well. Cover the pot and return to a boil. Stir again, partially cover, and cook for 3 to 4 minutes, stirring at least one more time, until the pasta is done to your taste and the potatoes are tender.

04 While the pasta and potatoes cook, add the basil, olive oil, ¼ cup cheese, pine nuts, and salt to taste to the food processor. Puree. Stop the motor of the food processor and scrape down the sides of the bowl with a rubber spatula. Just before the pasta is done, scoop out 1 cup of the cooking water. With the motor of the food processor running, gradually add the cooking water until fully incorporated.

05 Drain the cooked pasta and potatoes and put them in a large mixing bowl. Add the pesto mixture and toss well. Add a little more hot water (either from the remaining cooking water or from the hot-water tap) if needed to make the sauce coat more evenly. Add the tomatoes, toss again, and serve. Pass around additional grated cheese at the table, if desired.

Pasta with Broccoli Raab and Feta Cheese

SERVES:	4	FAT:	11.03g /26.65%
CALORIES:	366.55	SATURATED FAT:	3.68g

Unlike most kids in the '50s and '60s, I grew up loving bitter greens. Mom usually served them simply with olive oil and garlic. Now bitter greens are trendy (imagine that) and frequently served in restaurants, often with pasta. Broccoli raab (also known as *broccoli di rape* or rapini), is a nonheading variety of broccoli and the most common bitter green paired with pasta. Kale can be substituted for broccoli raab, and the more common cow's milk feta for sheep's milk feta.

1 bunch broccoli raab or kale (about 1 pound)

2 teaspoons salt plus additional for seasoning

12 ounces fresh short pasta such as fusilli or
     penne or dried capellini (angel hair)

1 cup fat-free, reduced-sodium chicken stock

4 cloves garlic

¾ teaspoon red pepper flakes, or to taste

2½ ounces feta cheese, preferably sheep's milk
     (about ¾ cup)

Freshly ground pepper

1½ tablespoons extra-virgin olive oil

Grated pecorino Romano cheese to pass
     at the table

01 Run the hot-water tap and put 2 quarts hot tap water in each of 2 pots (one large enough to eventually hold all the water, pasta, and broccoli raab). Cover and bring both pots to a boil over high heat, 8 to 10 minutes.

02 Meanwhile, cut off the bottom ½ inch from the bunch of broccoli raab and remove any withered or yellowed leaves. Then lay the bunch on its side on a cutting board. Cut the bunch crosswise beginning at the top. The leafy tops should be cut into ribbons about ¾ inch wide. The stem portions should be no more than ⅜ inch wide.

03 As soon as the water boils, pour the water from the smaller pot into the larger pot. Add the broccoli raab and the 2 teaspoons salt. Stir, cover and cook for 3 minutes. If using dried capellini, break in half. Add the pasta to the pot. Stir, cover, and return to a boil. Stir again, partially cover, and cook for 3 to 4 minutes, stirring at least one more time, until the pasta is done to your taste.

04 Meanwhile, put the chicken stock in a 12-inch sauté pan or Dutch oven over medium-high heat. Peel and chop the garlic. Add to the pan along with the red pepper flakes. Crumble or chop the feta.

05 When the broccoli raab and pasta are done, drain and add both to the sauté pan. Season to taste with salt and pepper. Toss to mix. Add the feta and the olive oil. Toss well and serve. Pass the grated pecorino Romano at the table.

Spaghetti Carbonara with Prosciutto and Peas

Prosciutto has so much flavor that just three ounces here make up for six ounces of bacon or pancetta in more traditional spaghetti carbonara recipes. Peas are not customary in this dish but they help transform it into a complete meal as well as adding color, flavor, and fiber.

Olive oil spray
3 ounces lean prosciutto, cut into thin, but not
   paper-thin, slices
4 cloves garlic
¼ cup dry white wine
½ cup egg substitute
½ cup grated Parmesan cheese plus additional
   to pass at the table
¾ cup 2-percent milk
¼ teaspoon ground nutmeg, preferably
   freshly grated
2 teaspoons salt plus additional for seasoning
Freshly ground pepper
12 ounces fresh spaghetti or dried capellini
   (angel hair)
1 cup frozen peas

01 Run the hot-water tap and put 2 quarts hot tap water in each of 2 pots (one large enough to eventually hold all the water and pasta). Cover and bring both pots to a boil over high heat, 8 to 10 minutes.

02 Meanwhile, spray a nonstick skillet with olive oil spray and put over medium heat. Cut the prosciutto crosswise into thin strips. Add to the skillet. Increase the heat to medium-high and cook for 1 minute while you peel and chop the garlic. Add the garlic to the pan. Stir and cook for 1 minute. Add the wine and cook for 1 minute while you beat the egg substitute, ½ cup cheese, milk, nutmeg, and salt and pepper to taste in a large mixing bowl or serving bowl. Add the contents of the skillet to the bowl.

03 When the pasta water boils, pour the water from the smaller pot into the larger pot and add the 2 teaspoons salt. Cut (if fresh) or break (if dried) the pasta in half and add to the pot. Add the peas. Stir well, cover, and return to a boil. Stir well again, partially cover, and cook for 3 to 4 minutes, stirring at least one more time, or until the pasta is done to your taste. Just before the pasta and peas are done, scoop out and reserve ⅓ cup of the cooking water.

04 When the pasta and peas are cooked, drain, leaving some water clinging to them. Add the pasta and peas to the mixing bowl and toss well. If the pasta looks dry, add some or all of the reserved pasta cooking water and toss well until the pasta is coated evenly with sauce. Serve in soup plates or pasta bowls. Garnish with a liberal grinding of black pepper. Pass additional cheese at the table.

Pasta with Three-Mushroom Sauce

The meaty quality of mushrooms helps to make this pasta dish a real rib sticker. Recipe tester Eugenia Gratto said, "Pasta dishes without meat often leave me hungry—but I walked away from the table full." Use whatever combination of mushrooms you like. The sauce is inspired by a recipe from Jack Czarnecki, chef and owner of the Joel Palmer House in Dayton, Oregon, and one of the most passionate mushroom aficionados in the United States.

1 tablespoon olive oil

1 small to medium onion (4 to 8 ounces)

2 cloves garlic

1½ pounds mixed mushrooms, such as shiitake, cremini, button, and oyster

1 tablespoon fresh thyme leaves or 1 teaspoon dried

5 sprigs parsley, preferably flat-leaf, or 5 chives

⅓ cup Marsala, dry sherry, or brandy

1 tablespoon soy sauce

Healthy pinch of sugar

2 cups fat-free, reduced-sodium chicken stock

2 teaspoons salt plus additional for seasoning

12 ounces dried capellini (angel hair) or any fresh pasta

4 teaspoons cornstarch

One 5-ounce can evaporated nonfat milk

Freshly ground pepper

Grated Parmesan cheese to pass at the table

01 Run the hot-water tap and put 2 quarts hot tap water in each of 2 pots (one large enough to eventually hold all the water and pasta). Cover and bring both pots to a boil over high heat, 8 to 10 minutes.

02 Meanwhile, put the oil in a 12-inch sauté pan over medium heat. Peel and quarter the onion. Peel the garlic. Put the onion and garlic into a food processor. Pulse just until chopped. (Or chop by hand.) Add to the sauté pan and stir. Thinly slice the mushrooms. (If using shiitake mushrooms, remove and discard the stems.) Add to the pan, raise the heat to high, and stir. Cook for 3 minutes.

03 Meanwhile, chop the thyme leaves. Chop the parsley leaves. Add the thyme, Marsala, soy sauce, sugar, and 1½ cups of the chicken stock to the sauté pan. Stir, cover, and bring to a boil. Reduce the heat to a simmer.

04 As soon as the pasta water boils, pour the water from the smaller pot into the larger pot. Add the 2 teaspoons salt and the pasta. Stir well, cover, and return to a boil. Stir well again, partially cover, and cook for 3 to 4 minutes, stirring at least one more time, or until the pasta is done to your taste.

05 Meanwhile, mix the cornstarch with the remaining ½ cup of chicken stock. Stir into the sauté pan. Cover and bring to a boil over high heat. Uncover, add the evaporated milk, and season with salt and pepper to taste. Stir and reduce heat to medium. Simmer while stirring periodically until the sauce thickens lightly. Do not boil. When the pasta is cooked, drain and divide among 4 individual soup plates. Pour sauce over each. Sprinkle with the chopped parsley and serve with Parmesan at the table.

Pasta Primavera

SERVES: 4	FAT: 9.02g /17.84%
CALORIES: 447.50	SATURATED FAT: 4.23g

Though *primavera* means spring in Italian, you can make this colorful pasta any time of the year. In fact, summer may be the best time when there is so much good local produce around. Because you have a great deal of flexibility with this dish, select the best vegetables the market has to offer that day. Other than those listed below, you could use broccoli, carrots, summer squash, and zucchini. Alternative herbs include chervil, chives, Italian parsley, oregano, tarragon, and thyme.

Olive oil spray
1 medium onion (about 8 ounces)
8 ounces button mushrooms
One 7-ounce jar roasted red bell peppers
2 teaspoons salt plus additional for seasoning
8 ounces asparagus or green beans
8 ounces sugar snap peas or snow peas
1 clove garlic
½ cup well-packed fresh basil leaves
1 cup part-skim ricotta
⅔ cup whole milk
½ teaspoon freshly ground pepper plus additional
    for seasoning
12 ounces any short fresh pasta such as penne or fusilli,
    or dried capellini (angel hair)
1 cup cherry tomatoes
Grated Parmesan cheese to pass at the table

01 Run the hot-water tap and put 2 quarts hot tap water in each of 2 pots (one large enough to eventually hold all the water, asparagus, peas, and pasta). Cover and bring both pots to a boil over high heat, 8 to 10 minutes.

02 Meanwhile, spray a 12-inch, nonstick sauté pan with olive oil spray and put it over medium heat. Cut off a thin slice from the top and bottom of the onion. Halve the onion lengthwise, then peel each half. Cut the halves crosswise into thin half-moon slices. Add the onion to the sauté pan. Thinly slice the mushrooms. Add to the sauté pan. Increase the heat to medium-high, stir, and cover. Drain the red bell peppers. Coarsely chop. Add to the sauté pan and stir. Season with salt to taste and cook the vegetables until they begin to soften but are still firm, about 3 minutes.

03 Meanwhile, cut off the bottom inch from the asparagus spears (or the tips of the green beans) and cut into 1-inch-long pieces. Break the stem ends off the sugar snap or snow peas and peel off the strings, if desired.

04 Peel the garlic. With the motor of a food processor running, drop the garlic down the chute to finely chop. Stop the motor and scrape down the sides with a rubber spatula. Add the basil leaves and pulse until chopped. Add the ricotta, milk, ½ teaspoon pepper, and salt to taste. Puree until smooth. Scrape into a large mixing or serving bowl. Add the vegetables from the sauté pan and mix well.

05 As soon as the pasta water boils, pour the water from the smaller pot into the larger pot. If using dried capellini, break the pasta in half. Add the pasta to the pot with the 2 teaspoons salt, the asparagus, and peas. Stir well, cover, and return to a boil. Stir well again, partially cover, and cook for 3 to 4 minutes, stirring at least one more time, or until the pasta is done to your taste.

06 Meanwhile, cut the cherry tomatoes in half and add to the mixing bowl. Just before the pasta and vegetables are done, scoop out and reserve ⅔ cup of the cooking water. Drain the cooked vegetables and pasta, leaving some water clinging to them. Add to the mixing bowl. Toss and gradually add the reserved pasta cooking water, ⅓ cup at a time, until the pasta is well coated with sauce. Adjust seasoning with additional salt and pepper, if necessary. Pass the Parmesan at the table.

Spaghetti all'Amatriciana

SERVES: 4

CALORIES: 505.44

FAT: 12.81g /23.48%

SATURATED FAT: 4.46g

Named for the town of Amatrice in the Sabine Hills outside Rome, this dish is an example of what good Italian cooking is all about: simplicity and good ingredients. Don't try to gussy it up. Let the sweet and low-acid San Marzano canned tomatoes come through loud and clear. San Marzano isn't a brand name but an area near Naples. Other quality Italian plum tomatoes may be substituted. Also important is the quality of bacon, or, if you prefer, pancetta, the Italian unsmoked bacon.

2 ounces bacon

1 medium onion (about 8 ounces)

½ cup dry red wine

One 28-ounce can imported San Marzano
   tomatoes

½ teaspoon red pepper flakes, or to taste

1 tablespoon salt plus additional for seasoning

Freshly ground black pepper

1 pound fresh spaghetti or dried capellini
   (angel hair)

4 sprigs parsley, preferably flat-leaf, enough
   for 2 tablespoons chopped

4 tablespoons grated pecorino Romano cheese
   plus additional to pass at the table

01   Run the hot-water tap and put 2 quarts hot tap water in each of 2 pots (one large enough to eventually hold all the water and pasta). Cover and bring both pots to a boil over high heat, 8 to 10 minutes.

02   Meanwhile, put a 12-inch sauté pan over medium heat. Cut the bacon into ¼- to ½-inch pieces. Add to the pan. Increase the heat to high. Stir, cover, and cook for 2 minutes. Meanwhile, peel the onion and chop in a food processor or by hand. Add to the sauté pan and cook, uncovered, for 2 minutes.

03   Add the wine to the sauté pan and cook for 1 minute. Meanwhile, coarsely puree the tomatoes in the food processor. Add the tomatoes with juices to the pan. Rinse out the tomato can with ⅓ cup water and add to the pan with the red pepper flakes and salt and black pepper to taste. Cover and bring to a boil. Uncover and reduce heat to a brisk simmer.

04   When the pasta water boils, transfer the water from the smaller pot into the larger pot. Add the pasta and the 1 tablespoon salt to the pot. Stir well, cover, and return to a boil. Stir well again, partially cover, and cook for 3 to 4 minutes, stirring at least one more time, or until the pasta is done to your taste.

05   Meanwhile, chop the parsley leaves and stir into the tomato sauce. When the pasta is cooked, drain, and divide among 4 soup plates or pasta bowls. Top with the tomato sauce and sprinkle each with 1 tablespoon of the cheese. Pass additional cheese at the table.

Pasta with Shrimp, Green Beans, and Lemon-Garlic Sauce

SERVES: 4

CALORIES: 538.05

FAT: 10.74G /17.99%

SATURATED FAT: 1.59G

Italians don't think you need oceans of sauce for your pasta to swim in. This dish is very Italian with just enough sauce to coat the pasta. It also has a nice balance of flavors from garlic, lemon, and dill. No cheese is needed.

One 8-ounce bottle clam juice

3 cloves garlic

1 pound shelled shrimp (21 to 24 per pound)

2 teaspoons salt plus additional for seasoning

Freshly ground black pepper

2 lemons

12 ounces string beans or haricot verts

12 ounces dried capellini (angel hair) or any fresh,
   short pasta such as penne or fusilli

½ cup pimientos or roasted red bell peppers from a jar

8 to 10 large sprigs fresh dill, enough for ¼ cup
   chopped leaves

2 tablespoons extra-virgin olive oil

Red pepper flakes (optional)

01 Run the hot-water tap and put 2 quarts hot tap water in each of 2 pots (one large enough to eventually hold all the water, pasta, and string beans). Cover and bring both pots to a boil over high heat, 8 to 10 minutes.

02 Meanwhile, put the clam juice in a 12-inch, nonstick sauté pan over high heat. Peel and chop the garlic. Remove the tails, if any, from the shrimp and cut each shrimp in half, crosswise. (Leave the shrimp whole if smaller.) Add the shrimp, garlic, and salt and black pepper to taste to the pan. Cook for 2 minutes, shaking the pan once or twice.

03 Meanwhile, zest the peel from one of the lemons with a lemon zester and finely chop it, or grate it with a grater. You should have about 2 teaspoons. Halve both lemons and juice them. Add the lemon juice and lemon zest to the pan with the shrimp, shake it a few times, and cook for 1 minute, then turn off the heat.

04 Meanwhile, trim the ends from the string beans and halve crosswise. (Keep whole if using haricot verts.) As soon as the pasta water boils, transfer the water from the smaller pot into the larger pot and add the 2 teaspoons salt. If using dried capellini, break the pasta in half. Put the string beans and pasta in the pot, stir well, cover, and return to a boil. Stir well again, partially cover, and cook for 3 to 4 minutes, stirring at least one more time, or until the beans and pasta are done to your taste. Just before the pasta is done, scoop out and reserve ½ cup of the cooking water.

05 While the pasta cooks, drain and coarsely chop the pimientos and add to the shrimp. Chop the dill and add to the shrimp. Drain the pasta and beans, leaving some water clinging to them, and add to the sauté pan. Add half of the reserved pasta cooking water, the olive oil, and red pepper flakes, if desired. Toss well. Add more salt and the remaining cooking water, if necessary. Toss again and serve.

Pasta with Tuna Sauce

SERVES:	4		FAT:	8.06g /16.55%
CALORIES:	440.83		SATURATED FAT:	1.38g

"Gutsy" is the best word to describe this robust pasta sauce that even anchovy haters—like my wife, Mary—will love. In addition, the dish is tailor-made for a well-stocked pantry. No meat, fish, or vegetables to pick up on the way home. Except for the pasta cooking water, no salt is added because many of the ingredients in the sauce are quite salty.

1 tablespoon extra-virgin olive oil

4 cloves garlic

3 canned anchovy fillets

One 28-ounce can or two 14.5-ounce cans diced
   or crushed tomatoes

¼ cup drained capers

10 large sprigs parsley, preferably flat-leaf,
   enough for ⅓ cup chopped leaves

12 ounces fresh pasta such as penne or fusilli,
   or dried capellini (angel hair)

2 teaspoons salt

Two 6-ounce cans albacore tuna in water

Freshly ground black pepper

Red pepper flakes

01 Run the hot-water tap and put 2 quarts hot tap water in each of 2 pots (one large enough to eventually hold all the water and pasta). Cover and bring both pots to a boil over high heat, 8 to 10 minutes.

02 Meanwhile, put the oil in a 12-inch, nonstick sauté pan over medium heat. Peel the garlic. With the motor of a food processor running, drop the garlic and anchovy fillets down the chute. (Or chop by hand.) When finely chopped, scrape into the sauté pan. Increase the heat to medium-high and cook for 2 minutes, stirring to prevent burning.

03 Meanwhile, open the can(s) of tomatoes. Add the tomatoes with juices and capers to the pan. Stir, cover, and bring to a boil while you chop the leaves of the parsley.

04 As soon as the pasta water boils, pour the water from the smaller pot into the larger pot. If using dried capellini, break the pasta in half. Add the pasta and the 2 teaspoons salt to the pot. Stir well, cover, and return to a boil. Stir well again, partially cover, and cook for 3 to 4 minutes, stirring at least one more time, or until the pasta is done to your taste. Just before the pasta is done, scoop out and reserve ½ cup of the cooking water.

05 While the pasta cooks, open the cans of tuna and add the tuna with juices to the tomato sauce. Add all but 2 teaspoons of the chopped parsley to the tomato sauce. Season with black pepper and red pepper flakes to taste. Drain the pasta and add to the sauté pan. Toss well and add the reserved cooking water as needed, ¼ cup at a time. Divide among 4 individual plates and sprinkle each with the remaining chopped parsley.

Soups and Stews

Soups and stews more easily camouflage the absence of fat than many other dishes by using stocks, milks, and juices. As recipe tester Mary Goad noted about the Curried Shrimp and Corn Chowder (page 103), which uses reduced-fat coconut milk, "It really gives you the feeling that you are eating a fatty cream soup." In addition to disguising fat that isn't there, liquids stretch out fatty ingredients that are there, like the ham in Black-Eyed Pea Soup with Collard Greens (page 111).

Moreover, soups and stews provide enormous flexibility, readily accepting substituted or new ingredients. Every cuisine has its repertoire and I've tried to represent as many ethnic persuasions as possible, from Spanish (Paella, page 101) to Asian (Asian Chicken Noodle Soup, page 113) to Louisianan (Crab and Oyster Gumbo, page 104).

You may be wondering, "Don't soups take a long time to make?" Yes, if you make them the traditional way. For example, if you made black bean soup by soaking dried black beans overnight, then simmering them for hours in homemade broth with a smoked pork hock. But who has time for that?

My soups make use of canned beans, one of the great convenience items in any pantry. I also use the best fat-free canned chicken stock I can find and a quality reduced-fat kielbasa. Put them together with flavor enhancers like sherry, garlic, cumin, and chipotle peppers, and the result is a fifteen-minute, low-fat soup that I'd stand up against many soups that took hours to make. Skeptical? Not Joyce Osborn, who tested the Black Bean Soup with Turkey Kielbasa (page 108): "This is a winner with my family," she said.

Quality canned and frozen foods are convenient, but you can't just rely on emptying cans into a pot. In this chapter, as in the rest of the book, I use fresh ingredients often, whether it is fresh collard greens in Black-Eyed Pea Soup with Collard Greens (page 111), fresh broccoli in Broccoli and Pasta Soup (page 102), or fresh bok choy in Asian Chicken Noodle Soup (page 113).

The most helpful piece of equipment for making fifteen-minute soups and stews is a sturdy, twelve-inch sauté pan with a nonstick surface. This deep skillet, which should have a capacity of four quarts or more, can make soup or stew for four to six people quickly because it combines a skillet with a soup pot.

Another trick is to heat the broth in a separate pot—ideally a wide saucepan that will heat the liquid quickly—while you sauté onion, garlic, and other vegetables in the sauté pan. When the vegetables are done and seasonings added, the hot broth is poured into the sauté pan, and the soup comes to a boil almost instantly.

Are these soups satisfying enough for a meal? A logical question. Kendra Knight's answer was typical of what testers told me. Of the Asian Chicken Noodle Soup (page 113) she said, "I thought maybe one serving wouldn't be filling enough but I was full and satisfied with one bowl." Main course soups and light stews afford us something satisfying without weighing us down, especially during the week, and particularly if we're trying to lose a few pounds.

Paella

SERVES: 4
CALORIES: 476.62

FAT: 8.69g /15.98%
SATURATED FAT: 3.05g

Imagine having this famous—and normally elaborate—Spanish dish on a weeknight. The key to making this paella work in a hurry is to cook the rice separately from the other ingredients almost until the very end. My choice of wine would be a fruity Spanish red that has some firmness to it, like a crianza from the Rioja region. *Ole!*

1 cup basmati rice
1 teaspoon salt plus additional for seasoning
½ teaspoon saffron threads
Olive oil spray
12 ounces boneless and skinless chicken breasts
1 medium onion (about 8 ounces)
3 to 4 cloves garlic
One 14.5-ounce can diced tomatoes
One 8-ounce bottle clam juice
½ pound turkey kielbasa
½ cup pimientos or roasted red bell peppers
    from a jar
1 teaspoon paprika
Freshly ground pepper
1 cup frozen peas
½ pound raw shelled shrimp (about 21 to 24
    per pound)

01 While the hot-water tap runs, put the rice, the 1 teaspoon salt, and ¼ teaspoon of the saffron, crushed between your fingers, in a 2-quart saucepan. Add 1⅔ cups hot tap water. Cover and bring to a boil over high heat. Reduce the heat to low and cook for 8 minutes. (Or put the rice, 1⅔ cups of hot tap water, the 1 teaspoon salt, and ¼ teaspoon of crushed saffron in a 2-quart, microwave-safe container. Cover and cook in a microwave oven on high power for 8 minutes.)

02 Meanwhile, spray a 12-inch, nonstick sauté pan with olive oil spray and put over medium heat. Cut the chicken into 1-inch pieces. Add to the sauté pan. Raise the heat to high and stir. Peel and quarter the onion. Peel the garlic. Put the onion and garlic into a food processor. Pulse just until chopped. (Or chop by hand.) Scrape into the sauté pan, stir, and cook for 2 minutes.

03 Meanwhile, open and drain the canned tomatoes. Open the bottle of clam juice. Cut the turkey kielbasa crosswise into ½-inch-thick pieces. Chop the pimientos. Add the drained tomatoes, clam juice, kielbasa, pimientos, paprika, the remaining ¼ teaspoon of saffron, crushed between your fingers, and salt and pepper to taste to the sauté pan. Cover and bring to a boil.

04 As soon as the liquid in the sauté pan comes to a boil, 1 to 2 minutes, add the peas and rice. Cover and bring to a boil again. Uncover and add the shrimp. Continue to boil, stirring periodically, just until the rice is tender and most or all of the liquid has been absorbed.

Broccoli and Pasta Soup

SERVES:	4	FAT:	7.34g /16.64%
CALORIES:	386.53	SATURATED FAT:	1.85g

Italians love soup, especially soup with vegetables and tiny pasta like *acini di pepe* or pastina. But they're not the only ones. Recipe tester Jennifer J. Hill said, "My 4 year-old daughter, who does not like soup or vegetables, ate it." As befits the Southern Italian nature of this dish, I use pecorino Romano instead of Parmesan. It has a sharper flavor, which is more appropriate for the rustic quality of the soup. You could also make this recipe with broccoli raab or other hearty greens.

8 cups fat-free, reduced-sodium chicken stock
4 cloves garlic
1 bunch broccoli or about 1½ pounds
   broccoli florets
¾ cup acini di pepe, pastina, or other very
   small pasta
One 15-ounce can cannellini beans
Salt
¼ teaspoon (or more) freshly ground pepper
4 tablespoons grated pecorino Romano cheese
4 teaspoons extra-virgin olive oil

01 Put the stock in a 12-inch sauté pan over high heat and cover. Peel the garlic. With the motor of a food processor running, drop the garlic down the chute and finely chop. Add to the chicken stock, stir, and cover.

02 Remove and peel the stems of the broccoli and quarter each stem crosswise. Break the heads into florets. Peel any parts of the florets that look tough. Put half the broccoli into the food processor and pulse until you get a coarse puree. Move the broccoli around in the bowl of the processor with a rubber scraper or wooden spoon so it will chop evenly. Scrape the chopped broccoli into a bowl. Repeat the process with the remaining broccoli.

03 Add the broccoli to the sauté pan and cover. When the stock comes to a boil, add the pasta. Cover and bring to a boil again. Reduce the heat to medium and cook, partially covered, about 7 minutes or just until the broccoli and pasta are tender.

04 Meanwhile, open the can of beans into a colander. Rinse briefly. Add to the pan and season the soup with salt to taste and ¼ teaspoon or more of pepper. Stir, cover, and cook just until the soup is heated through. Divide the soup among 4 soup plates. Sprinkle a tablespoon of cheese over each, then drizzle each with a teaspoon of olive oil.

Curried Shrimp and Corn Chowder

SERVES: 4	FAT: 8.71g /21.25%
CALORIES: 353.25	SATURATED FAT: 3.65g

Chowders don't have to have clams or potatoes—or come from New England. With coconut milk, curry, and cilantro, this soup is as far from clam chowder as Boston is from Bangkok. I can't resist using fresh local corn when it's in season, but canned and frozen corn work quite well.

Canola oil spray
1 medium onion (about 8 ounces)
2 cloves garlic
1 pound peeled raw shrimp (about 21 to 24 per pound)
1 tablespoon curry powder
1 cup reduced-fat coconut milk
3 cups 1-percent milk
3 large or 4 medium ears fresh corn or 2 cups frozen or canned corn kernels
¼ teaspoon (or more) cayenne pepper
Salt
Freshly ground black pepper
⅓ cup fresh cilantro leaves

01　Spray a 12-inch, nonstick sauté pan with canola oil spray and put over medium heat. Peel and quarter the onion. Peel the garlic. Put the onion and the garlic into a food processor. Pulse just until chopped. (Or chop by hand.) Scrape into the pan, raise the heat to medium-high, and stir.

02　Remove the tails from the shrimp, if any, and cut in half crosswise. Add to the pan and stir. Stir in the curry powder. Cook for 1 minute. Add the coconut milk and 1-percent milk. Stir and cover.

03　Husk the corn. To remove the kernels, stand each cob on end and, beginning at the middle, cut down all around the cob. Then reverse the ends and repeat. (If using frozen corn, empty the box into a colander and let hot tap water run over for 1 to 2 minutes until defrosted. If using canned corn, drain in a colander.) Add the kernels to the pan. Take the back of a chef's knife and rub it against the cobs over the pan to remove the flavorful "milk."

04　Add ¼ teaspoon cayenne pepper, and salt and black pepper to taste, to the pan. Stir and cover until the soup comes to a simmer, about 4 minutes. Do not boil.

05　Meanwhile, chop the cilantro leaves. Add to the soup, and cook for 1 minute. Add more cayenne pepper, if desired, and serve.

Crab and Oyster Gumbo

Gumbo and its Creole cousin, jambalaya, are rich and spicy Louisiana rice dishes with many variations that may contain andouille sausage, chicken, even rabbit. Gumbo is soupier than jambalaya and normally flavored with a long, slow-cooked roux of fat and flour, which time and calories don't permit here. Filé powder, which many supermarkets now carry, is a seasoning and thickener made from the leaves of the sassafras tree. (See page 149 for mail-order sources.) Thyme and bay leaves may be substituted.

1 cup basmati rice

1 teaspoon salt plus additional for seasoning

Canola oil spray

3 cloves garlic

1 medium onion (about 8 ounces)

1 rib celery

1 small to medium green bell pepper

One 10-ounce package frozen cut okra

One 14.5-ounce can stewed tomatoes

Two 8-ounce bottles clam juice

2 teaspoons gumbo filé powder (or 1 teaspoon dried thyme and 2 bay leaves)

¼ teaspoon (or more) cayenne pepper

Freshly ground black pepper

2 dozen shucked oysters with their liquor (juice)

8 ounces jumbo lump crab meat

01   While the hot-water tap runs, put the rice in a 2-quart saucepan. Add 2 cups hot tap water and the 1 teaspoon salt. Cover and bring to a boil over high heat, then reduce the heat to low and cook for 10 minutes. (Or put the rice, 2 cups hot tap water, and the 1 teaspoon salt in a 2-quart, microwave-safe container. Cover and cook in microwave oven on high power for 10 minutes.)

02   Meanwhile, spray a 12-inch, nonstick sauté pan with canola oil spray and put over medium heat. Peel the garlic. With the motor of a food processor running, drop the garlic down the chute and finely chop. Peel and quarter the onion. Trim and quarter the celery. Put the onion and celery into the food processor. Pulse just until chopped. (Or chop by hand.) Add the garlic, onion, and celery to the pan, stir, and raise the heat to high.

03   Cut the top from the bell pepper. Stand the pepper upright and cut down inside the pepper's four walls, separating them from the center core and seeds. Put the walls of the bell pepper into the food processor and pulse just until coarsely chopped. (Or chop by hand.) Add to the pan and stir. Cut the frozen block of okra in quarters and put in a colander under hot running water to defrost.

04   Open the stewed tomatoes and put into the food processor. Pulse briefly. Add the tomatoes to the pan along with the clam juice, filé powder, ¼ teaspoon cayenne pepper, and salt and black pepper to taste. Stir well. Add the okra. Cover and bring to a boil, about 2 minutes.

05   Meanwhile, pour the oysters and their liquor in a shallow bowl and pick out any bits of shell. Uncover the sauté pan and break up any clumps of frozen okra. Add the oysters, their liquor, and the crab meat. Cover and return to a boil. Uncover, reduce the heat, and simmer for about 4 minutes or until the soup is lightly thickened and the okra is cooked and completely separate. Add more cayenne pepper, if desired. To serve, divide the cooked rice among 4 soup plates and top with the gumbo.

Hearty Minestrone

SERVES: 4
CALORIES: 307.12

FAT: 7.86g /21.99%
SATURATED FAT: 1.79g

I couldn't believe how delicious and satisfying this soup was when I first made it. I didn't feel like having anything else with it, though some hearty Italian bread isn't a bad idea. The soup easily becomes a vegetarian dish by substituting vegetable stock for chicken stock, and vegan-friendly by eliminating the cheese. For more flavor, add the rind from the Parmesan to the stock.

6 cups fat-free, reduced-sodium chicken stock
Rind from a piece of Parmesan (optional)
Olive oil spray
3 cloves garlic
1 medium onion (about 8 ounces)
1 medium carrot
8 ounces string beans
8 ounces zucchini
One 15-ounce can small white beans such as navy
　　or Great Northern
One 15-ounce can diced tomatoes
2 ounces capellini (angel hair) pasta
One 10-ounce bag washed, fresh spinach
12 large fresh basil leaves
Salt
Freshly ground pepper
4 tablespoons grated Parmesan cheese
4 teaspoons extra-virgin olive oil

01 Put the stock in a wide saucepan over high heat. Add the Parmesan rind, if desired. Cover and bring to a boil. Meanwhile, spray a 12-inch, nonstick sauté pan or Dutch oven with olive oil spray and put over medium heat. Peel the garlic. Peel and quarter the onion. Peel and quarter the carrot. Put the garlic, onion, and carrot into a food processor. Pulse until coarsely chopped. (Or chop by hand.) Add to the sauté pan. Stir and cook for 2 minutes.

02 Meanwhile, trim the string beans and cut them in half crosswise, or thirds if large. Add the chicken stock and string beans to the sauté pan. Stir, cover, and bring to a boil over high heat.

03 Meanwhile, trim the zucchini, cut in half lengthwise, then cut crosswise into thin half moons. Drain the can of beans into a colander. Rinse briefly. Open the can of tomatoes. Break the capellini in thirds. Add the zucchini, beans, tomatoes with juices, and capellini to the sauté pan. Stir, cover, and return to a boil over high heat.

04 Meanwhile, pick through the spinach, discarding any withered leaves and thick stems. Coarsely chop and add to the pan. Stack the basil leaves, roll in cigar fashion, and cut crosswise into ribbons. Add to the pan along with salt and pepper to taste. Stir well, cover, and return to a boil over high heat for a few minutes or until the vegetables are tender.

05 Divide the soup among 4 soup plates and top each with 1 tablespoon of grated cheese. Drizzle a teaspoon of olive oil on top of each.

Black Bean Soup with Turkey Kielbasa

SERVES: 4

CALORIES: 401.18

FAT: 7.29g /17.74%

SATURATED FAT: 2.70g

I'm not sure why, but black beans, especially black bean soup, and sherry always seem to go well together. So do beans and hot peppers. Chipotle peppers are smoked jalapeño peppers. Dried chipotles can be purchased at specialty shops or by mail (see page 149). More mainstream supermarkets are starting to carry chipotles in adobo sauce in small cans. Cayenne pepper, red pepper flakes, or hot sauce like Tabasco can be substituted.

5½ cups fat-free, reduced-sodium chicken stock

½ cup dry sherry

Canola oil spray

1 medium onion (about 8 ounces)

3 cloves garlic

1 green bell pepper

1 medium to large carrot

Three 15-ounce cans black beans

3 to 4 teaspoons ground cumin

¼ to ½ teaspoon ground chipotle pepper, cayenne pepper, red pepper flakes, or hot pepper sauce like Tabasco

8 ounces turkey kielbasa

Salt

3 tablespoons fresh cilantro leaves

½ cup nonfat yogurt

01   Combine the chicken stock and sherry in a wide sauce-pan. Cover and put over high heat. Spray a 12-inch, nonstick sauté pan with canola oil spray and put over medium heat. Peel and quarter the onion. Peel the garlic. Put the onion and the garlic into a food processor. Pulse just until chopped. (Or chop by hand.) Scrape into the sauté pan, raise the heat to high, and stir.

02   Cut the top from the bell pepper. Stand the pepper upright and cut down inside the pepper's four walls, separating them from the center core and seeds. Put the pepper walls into the food processor. Trim the ends of the carrot, peel, and cut crosswise into 4 roughly equal pieces. Put into the food processor and pulse just until the pepper and carrot are coarsely chopped. (Or chop by hand.) Add to the pan. Stir.

03   Open the cans of beans into a colander. Rinse briefly and let drain. Add the cumin and chipotle pepper to the vegetables in the sauté pan and stir. Add the beans and the chicken stock mixture. Stir, cover, and bring to a boil, about 2 minutes.

04   Meanwhile, quarter the kielbasa lengthwise. Then cut crosswise into pieces $\frac{1}{2}$ to $\frac{3}{8}$ inch wide. With a potato masher or the back of a large spoon, mash one-quarter to one-third of the beans (depending on how thick you want the soup).

05   Add the kielbasa and salt to taste. Stir, cover, and return the soup to a boil. Meanwhile, chop the cilantro leaves. When the soup has come to a boil, uncover, and lower the heat to a brisk simmer. Cook for 3 minutes, stirring once or twice. Ladle the soup into bowls. Top with yogurt and sprinkle with cilantro.

Tortilla Soup

SERVES: 4
CALORIES: 380.26

FAT: 7.73g /17.63%
SATURATED FAT: 1.53g

This soup is amazingly easy and quite delicious. If you can't get the larger 19-ounce can of chickpeas, the smaller 15-ounce can will do just fine. And if you have some fresh corn on hand and want to spend a few minutes more on the dish, by all means use it. Add the fresh corn when you add the chickpeas.

Six 6-inch corn tortillas
Canola oil spray
6 cups fat-free, reduced-sodium chicken stock
2 cloves garlic
1 medium onion (about 8 ounces)
1 rib celery
One 19-ounce can chickpeas
One 4.5-ounce can chopped mild green chiles
2 teaspoons chili powder
1 cup frozen corn kernels
12 ounces smoked turkey breast
⅓ cup fresh cilantro leaves
Salt

01 Turn the oven to 500 degrees F. Stack the tortillas and cut in half. Then cut each half crosswise into ¼-inch-wide strips. Spray a sheet pan with canola oil spray and lay the tortilla strips out evenly on the sheet pan. Spray the tortilla strips with canola oil spray. Bake for 7 minutes. Meanwhile, put the chicken stock in a wide saucepan, cover, and put over high heat.

02 Spray a 12-inch, nonstick sauté pan with canola oil spray and put over medium heat. Peel the garlic. Peel and quarter the onion. Trim and quarter the celery. Put the onion, garlic, and celery into a food processor. Pulse just until chopped. (Or chop by hand.) Scrape into the sauté pan, raise the heat to high, and stir.

03 Open the can of chickpeas into a colander. Rinse briefly and let drain. Open the can of chiles. Add the chili powder to the sauté pan and stir. Add the chiles and their juices, corn, and chicken stock. Stir, cover, and bring to a boil.

04 Meanwhile, cut the turkey into ½-inch dice. Add the turkey and chickpeas to the sauté pan. Stir, cover, and bring to a boil. Reduce heat to a simmer.

05 Meanwhile, turn the tortilla strips over with a spatula and spray again with canola oil spray. Bake for 6 minutes more or until crisp. Chop the cilantro leaves and add half to the soup. Season to taste with salt. Ladle the soup into soup plates. Top with the tortilla strips and the remaining cilantro.

Black-Eyed Pea Soup with Collard Greens

SERVES: 4
CALORIES: 306.22

FAT: 3.81g /11%
SATURATED FAT: 1.00g

Beans and greens are a satisfying combination and highly nutritious. Southerners and African-Americans up North are used to cooking collards and greens like kale for hours. However, we're now able to get younger and more tender greens from farmers' markets as well as mainstream supermarkets, so they cook much quicker. If you can't get these fresh greens, use frozen greens. Black-eyed peas are also available frozen, but they take longer to cook than canned peas.

6 cups fat-free, reduced-sodium chicken stock
3 bay leaves
1 small bunch of tender collard greens or kale
**   (about 12 ounces) or one 10-ounce frozen**
**   package of collard greens or kale**
Canola oil spray
1 medium onion (about 8 ounces)
3 cloves garlic
6 ounces lean, smoked ham
Two 15-ounce cans black-eyed peas
Hot pepper sauce (such as Tabasco)
Salt
Freshly ground black pepper

01 Put the chicken stock in a wide saucepan over high heat. Add the bay leaves and cover.

02 Lay the bunch of fresh greens on its side on a cutting board. Cut off and discard the stems where the leaves begin. Remove any withered or yellowed leaves. Roll the leaves tightly and cut crosswise into strips no more than ½ inch wide. Add the greens to the chicken stock and cover. (If using frozen greens, cut the block of frozen greens into 8 or more pieces and add to the pan.)

03 Spray a 12-inch, nonstick sauté pan with canola oil spray and put over medium heat. Peel and quarter the onion. Peel the garlic. Put the onion and the garlic into a food processor. Pulse just until chopped. Dice the ham. Add the onion, garlic, and ham to the sauté pan, raise the heat to high, and stir. Cook for 2 minutes.

04 Meanwhile, open the cans of black-eyed peas into colander. Rinse briefly and let drain. Add the chicken stock and greens to the sauté pan. Stir and cover. Bring to a boil over high heat. Add the black-eyed peas to the pan and stir. Cover and bring to a boil.

05 Reduce heat to a brisk simmer. Season with hot pepper sauce to taste. Add salt and black pepper to taste. Cook for 4 minutes or until the greens are just tender. Remove the bay leaves and serve.

Asian Chicken Noodle Soup

SERVES: 4

CALORIES: 296.37

FAT: 5.53g /18.47%

SATURATED FAT: .90g

You don't need to wait to have a cold to make this chicken noodle soup, though you'll probably feel better after eating it. It's light but very satisfying. The secret ingredient is fish sauce, which is available at Asian and gourmet markets, though more supermarkets are carrying it. Consult the mail-order sources (page 149) if you can't find it locally.

5½ cups fat-free, reduced-sodium chicken stock

½ cup rice wine or dry sherry

2 ounces rice noodles (rice sticks)

Canola oil spray

One 2-inch piece fresh ginger

1 bunch green onions (scallions)

4 ounces shiitake mushrooms or
    button mushrooms

8 ounces boneless and skinless chicken
    breasts or chicken tenders

12 ounces bok choy (preferably baby bok choy)
    or napa cabbage

8 ounces mung bean sprouts

One 8-ounce can sliced water chestnuts

2 tablespoons fish sauce

Salt

Freshly ground pepper

1 tablespoon Asian sesame oil

01 Put the chicken stock and rice wine in a wide saucepan. Cover and put over high heat. Run the hot-water tap while you break the noodles in half. Put the noodles in a medium bowl and cover with hot tap water.

02 Spray a 12-inch, nonstick sauté pan with canola oil spray and put over medium heat. Peel and halve the ginger. With the motor of a food processor running, drop the ginger down the chute and finely chop. Trim the bulb ends of the green onions. Remove the green parts and set aside. Put the white parts into the food processor and pulse just until chopped. Add the ginger and onion mixture to the sauté pan, raise the heat to high, and stir.

03 Remove the stems from the shiitake mushrooms (leave stems on if using button mushrooms) and thinly slice the caps. Add to the sauté pan and stir. Cut the chicken into ½-inch cubes and add to the sauté pan. As soon as the chicken stock mixture has come to a boil, add it to the sauté pan and stir well. Cover and bring to a boil over high heat.

04 Meanwhile, quickly wash your knife, hands, and cutting board with soapy water and rinse. Cut the tops of the bok choy crosswise into ½-inch-wide ribbons. As you go farther down to the thicker stem, cut strips ¼ inch wide. Discard the bottom ½ inch. Drain the noodles. When the soup has returned to a boil, add the bok choy, noodles, and bean sprouts. Cover and return to a boil, about 1 minute.

05 Meanwhile, open and drain the can of water chestnuts. Add the water chestnuts and fish sauce to the soup. Season with salt and pepper to taste. Stir, cover, and cook for 2 minutes or until the noodles are tender. Finely chop the green parts of the onions. Remove the soup from the heat. Stir in the sesame oil. Ladle the soup into individual soup plates. Sprinkle with the green onions and serve.

It's almost axiomatic that people eat more salads when they are watching their weight. But they often don't take into account how much fat and how many calories are in the dressings they use. On the other hand, if they go the squeeze-of-lemon route, it's not terribly satisfying, which is one reason why I think people fall off the diet wagon.

In a way, salads are the reverse of soups and stews: They can't hide fat easily. So you've got to be more creative. Cutting down on fats, primarily the oils in dressings, without making the dressing seem thin or acidic is one of the keys.

The normal ratio of three or four parts oil to one part vinegar in a standard vinaigrette won't do for low-fat salads because each tablespoon of oil contains fourteen grams of fat. So in no time your fat allotment has been used up. Just adding more vinegar usually makes the salad too harsh or vinegary. One solution is to use vinegars with lower acidity.

Many of the vinegars people normally use in salads have an acidity of 6 or 7 percent. The idea is to get below 6 percent, preferably below 5 percent. Fruit vinegars such as the raspberry vinegar in Warm Chicken Curry Salad (page 122) often fall into this category. Some fruit vinegars, like those made by Consorzio, have so much fruit flavor and so little acidity, you can almost reverse the normal oil-vinegar ratio. Cider vinegars, which are technically fruit vinegars, are also low in acidity. They are used in several dishes in this chapter, including the Warm Potato Salad with Smoked Salmon and Cabbage (page 117). Rice wine vinegars typically have low acidity and are good when neutral flavors are called for— and not necessarily in Asian dishes. Balsamic vinegars are also mild with a touch of sweetness.

Citrus juices, especially lemon and lime juice, are excellent alternatives to fat. When I first tested the Taco Salad (page 130), I was a little over the fat limit. I cut the oil by a third and doubled the lime juice. The result was not only lower fat, but better taste. When oils are used, it is absolutely crucial that they be the most flavorful possible. Yes, they will be more expensive, but don't forget, you're only using a tablespoon or two.

Other fat substitutes in dressings include vegetable juices; stocks or broths, including the liquid from canned tuna, as in Tuna and White Beans with Bitter Greens (page 118); and wine or spirits, like the tequila used in the Taco Salad (page 130).

For creamy dressings such as those used for the Beef and Beet Salad with Horseradish Cream Dressing (page 128) and the Cobb Salad (page 123), low-fat or nonfat yogurt or sour cream, and low-fat buttermilk are very good choices.

Because dressings must be added carefully, every drop counts. For this reason, it's critical to have the ingredients that are to be dressed as dry as possible. If not, the dressing will not cling to them adequately. That's why a salad spinner is such an important piece of equipment.

I find the food processor indispensable in making quick salads. It rapidly makes salad dressings and slices or shreds vegetables. Some of my testers have told me it's just as fast to use a knife. I don't think so, and I'm a pretty fast chopper. Of course, sharp knives are always important, even with a food processor on hand.

Trying to mix a salad quickly and efficiently in a bowl that's too small is like trying to get into the dress (or tuxedo) you wore for your senior prom. If you don't have a large mixing bowl—and I mean large enough to bathe an infant—a large cooking pot will suffice.

Buying already shredded or sliced vegetables is another time-saver. Since my last book, *Cooking to Beat the Clock*, more and more of these products have appeared in supermarket produce sections, from hearts of romaine to ready-to-dress coleslaw mixes to sliced mushrooms. And don't forget the cut-up vegetables on the salad bar.

Think of the salads in this chapter like the pasta throw-togethers I mentioned in the Pasta chapter (page 79). Consider your whole pantry when choosing ingredients for your main-course salad, including leftovers from last night's dinner. But beware of the kitchen-sink mentality. Just because it's there doesn't mean it will work in a salad. For example, an opened jar of salsa might fit into a variation on the Taco Salad (page 130), but I'm not sure it would be appropriate in the Greek Bread Salad (page 126).

Another way to create main-course salads on your own is to start with some protein as the centerpiece, such as chicken breasts, salmon, or canned beans. Then build the salad around it as in the Warm Chicken Curry Salad (page 122), Warm Potato Salad with Smoked Salmon and Cabbage (page 117), or Tuna and White Beans with Bitter Greens (page 118). Or you could do the reverse. Take a salad that isn't a main-course salad and bulk it up to make it a meal. That's what I did in the Greek Bread Salad with Feta Cheese (page 126), which is never a main course in Greek restaurants.

Warm Potato Salad with Smoked Salmon and Cabbage

SERVES: 4
CALORIES: 297.36

FAT: 7.28g / 22.07%
SATURATED FAT: 2.56g

Cured or smoked salmon is so flavorful that a small amount goes a long way in salads and pastas. In this dish I use kippered salmon, which is cured or smoked salmon that has been baked, giving it a totally different flavor from normal smoked salmon. But smoked salmon can also be used in its place, as well as leftover baked, broiled, or poached salmon.

2 large red-skinned potatoes (about 1 pound)
1 teaspoon salt plus additional for seasoning
10 ounces green cabbage
4 ounces sweet onion such as Vidalia or red onion
1 small to medium red bell pepper
½ cup low-fat sour cream
¼ cup cider vinegar
1 tablespoon Dijon mustard
8 to 10 large sprigs fresh dill, enough for ¼ cup
   of chopped leaves
Freshly ground pepper
1 pound kippered or other smoked salmon
   or leftover baked or poached salmon

01 Halve the potatoes lengthwise, then thinly slice crosswise. (Do not peel.) While the hot-water tap runs, put the potatoes and the 1 teaspoon salt in a large saucepan. Barely cover with hot tap water. Put over high heat and cover. Cook for 10 minutes or until just tender.

02 Meanwhile, thinly shred the cabbage with a chef's knife, the large holes of a four-sided grater, or the slicing or shredding attachment of a food processor. You should have about 3 cups. Put the cabbage into a large mixing bowl.

03 Cut off a thin slice from the top and bottom of the onion, halve lengthwise, peel each half, and cut crosswise into thin half-moon slices. Add to the cabbage. Cut the top from the bell pepper. Stand the pepper upright and cut down inside the pepper's four walls, separating them from the center core and seeds. Then cut the pepper walls crosswise into thin strips. Add to the mixing bowl and mix all the ingredients well.

04 Put the sour cream, vinegar, and Dijon mustard in a small bowl. Chop the dill leaves. Add the dill and salt and pepper to taste to the sour cream mixture and stir well. Add the dressing to the vegetables. Mix well.

05 When the potatoes are done, drain them in a colander. Dry quickly with paper towels. Meanwhile, flake the salmon, removing any bones. Toss the potatoes with the other vegetables. Gently fold in the salmon.

Tuna and White Beans with Bitter Greens

SERVES: 4
CALORIES: 339.77

FAT: 9.45g /24.36%
SATURATED FAT: 1.34g

Tuna and beans provide a marvelous combination of protein and low-fat, as long as you use water-packed tuna. The quality of tuna varies dramatically from one brand to another, as a taste test done by the *New York Times* found out a few years ago. So experiment to find the one you like. Albacore tuna has a milder, less fishy taste and smell than other types of canned tuna, which are not normally listed by name.

1 bunch arugula

1 small head curly endive (8 to 10 ounces)

1 head radicchio (about 6 ounces)

Two 15-ounce cans cannellini or other white beans

4 ounces red onion or sweet onion such as Vidalia

8 sprigs parsley, preferably flat-leaf

¼ cup capers, drained

Two 6-ounce cans albacore tuna packed in water

1½ lemons

2 tablespoons extra-virgin olive oil

Salt

Freshly ground pepper

01 Fill the sink with cold water while you remove any withered or yellowed leaves from the greens. Cut the arugula crosswise into ¾-inch-wide strips, discarding the stems. Cut the endive crosswise into ¾-inch-wide strips, discarding the bottom 1 inch. Cut off and discard the bottom ½ inch from the radicchio. Halve the remainder lengthwise and, with the flat side down, cut each half lengthwise into ½-inch-wide strips. Wash the salad greens briefly but vigorously in the sink to remove grit. Spin dry in a salad spinner. Remove any excess moisture with paper towels.

02 While the greens dry, open the cans of beans into a colander. Rinse and let drain. Cut off a thin slice from the top and bottom of the onion, halve lengthwise, peel each half, and cut crosswise into thin half-moon slices. Chop the parsley leaves. Put the beans, onion, parsley, and capers in a large mixing bowl along with the salad greens.

03 Open the cans of tuna into the colander over a small bowl to catch the drained liquid. Flake the tuna and add to the mixing bowl.

04 Juice the lemons. Add the lemon juice to the drained tuna liquid along with the olive oil and salt and pepper to taste. Mix well and pour over the ingredients in the salad bowl. Toss well and serve.

Seafood Salad

SERVES: 4
CALORIES: 261.14

FAT: 7.39g /26.42%
SATURATED FAT: 1.48g

This salad is so creamy and rich tasting it's hard to believe it has only 7.39 grams of fat and 261 calories per serving. You can use almost any variety of seafood you like, from crab and lobster (if you're feeling a bit flush) to firm white fish. Other vegetables can include fennel, carrots, and cucumbers.

½ cup dry white wine or ¼ cup dry vermouth
8 ounces shelled raw shrimp (about 21 to 24 per pound)
8 ounces cleaned squid
8 ounces scallops
3 ribs celery
½ cup roasted peppers or pimientos from a jar
1 shallot
1 lemon
¼ cup light mayonnaise
½ cup nonfat or low-fat yogurt
Salt
Freshly ground black pepper
Cayenne pepper
4 cups gourmet salad mix
8 to 10 large sprigs fresh dill, enough for ¼ cup leaves
1 cup cherry tomatoes

01 Put the wine and 1 cup water in a 12-inch skillet. Put over high heat and cover. Meanwhile, remove the tails, if any, from the shrimp and cut the shrimp in half, crosswise. Cut the squid bodies crosswise into ½-inch-wide rings. Remove the strips or "hinges" from the scallops and halve. Quarter if especially large. When the liquid in the skillet boils, add the seafood, cover, and cook for 3 minutes.

02 Meanwhile, cut the celery crosswise into ½-inch-wide crescents. Chop the roasted pepper. Put both into a large mixing bowl. When the seafood is done, drain in a small colander. Then put in a bowl, and stick in the freezer to cool briefly.

03 While the seafood cools, peel and halve the shallot. With the motor of a food processor running, drop the shallot down the chute and finely chop. Scrape down the sides of the bowl with a rubber spatula. Juice the lemon and add to the processor along with the mayonnaise, yogurt, and salt, black pepper, and cayenne pepper to taste. Pulse briefly to mix well.

04 Put the salad greens in a salad spinner and fill with cold water. Drain and spin dry. Wrap in paper towels to remove excess moisture. While salad greens dry, chop the dill, and halve the cherry tomatoes.

05 Put the greens on a large platter. Add the dill, seafood, and the dressing to the mixing bowl with the celery and bell pepper. Combine well. Taste and add more salt, black pepper, and cayenne pepper, if necessary. Put the seafood mixture on the greens and place the tomatoes around the outside of the platter.

Warm Chicken Curry Salad

SERVES: 4	**FAT:** 11.10g /28.52%
CALORIES: 354.14	**SATURATED FAT:** 2.22g

This salad has a lot of flavors and textures that make it fun to put together and eat. It also has a great deal of flexibility. Instead of apples you could use pears, cantaloupe, or grapes. Dried fruits like raisins, dates, or apricots could be added as well. Turkey or pork tenderloin are possible substitutions for chicken. With any of these variations, I'd drink an off-dry wine such as a Riesling, Gewürztraminer, or Chenin Blanc.

1 tablespoon peanut or canola oil

1½ pounds boneless and skinless chicken breast halves or chicken tenders

Salt

2½ teaspoons high-quality curry powder such as Madras

1 small head romaine lettuce (about 1 pound)

¼ cup fat-free, reduced-sodium chicken stock

4 medium green onions (scallions)

⅓ cup fresh cilantro leaves

1 large, crisp apple such as a Fuji or Braeburn

½ cup plain, nonfat yogurt

¼ cup light mayonnaise

1 tablespoon honey

1 tablespoon raspberry or cider vinegar

01 Put the oil in a 12-inch, nonstick skillet over medium heat. Cut the chicken into 1-inch cubes. Season with salt, add to the skillet, and increase the heat to medium-high. Stir and cook for 1 minute. Sprinkle 2 teaspoons of the curry powder over the chicken and stir. Cook for 2 minutes.

02 Meanwhile, cut ½ inch from the top and bottom of the romaine and cut the head crosswise into 1-inch-wide strips. Put the strips in a salad spinner and fill with water. Drain and spin dry. Wrap in paper towels to remove excess moisture.

03 While the romaine is drying, add the chicken stock to the skillet. Bring to a boil over high heat, stirring well with a wooden spoon. Cook, uncovered, for 4 minutes or until no pink remains inside the chicken. Remove the pan from the heat.

04 While the chicken cooks, trim the green onions and cut the white and green parts crosswise into thin slices. Put in a large mixing bowl. Chop the cilantro and add to the bowl. Chop the apple by sitting it upright on a cutting board and cutting straight down on four sides around the core. (Do not peel.) Cut into ½-inch cubes. Add to the mixing bowl. Add the romaine to the mixing bowl.

05 Combine the remaining ½ teaspoon of curry powder, the yogurt, mayonnaise, honey, and vinegar in a small bowl. Put the chicken in the mixing bowl. Add the dressing and salt to taste. Toss well and serve.

Cobb Salad

SERVES: 4	FAT: 8.88g /31.28%
CALORIES: 248.10	SATURATED FAT: 4.38g

You're probably wondering how bacon fits into a low-fat recipe. The answer is, very carefully. But trust me, turkey bacon doesn't get it done here. While the fat grams are just fine in this salad, the percentage of fat is over 30 percent simply because there just aren't that many calories. If you want to add some fatless calories to bring that percentage down, consider grated carrots, canned beets, or cooked potatoes. Or leave it as is, which is what I'd do.

1 ounce bacon

1 medium to large head romaine lettuce (about 1 pound)

2 large tomatoes (14 to 16 ounces total)

2 green onions (scallions)

2 ounces blue cheese

⅓ cup low-fat buttermilk

⅓ cup nonfat plain yogurt

2 tablespoons cider vinegar

½ teaspoon Worcestershire sauce

⅛ teaspoon (or more) cayenne pepper

¼ teaspoon (or more) freshly ground black pepper

Salt

12 ounces smoked chicken or turkey breast, or cooked, unsmoked turkey or chicken breast

One 14-ounce can artichoke hearts in water

01 Put the bacon in a skillet over medium heat and cook on one side for 3 minutes.

02 While the bacon cooks, cut ½ inch from the top and bottom of the romaine and cut the head crosswise into 1-inch-wide strips. Put the strips in a salad spinner and fill with water. Drain and spin dry. Wrap in paper towels to remove excess moisture. Dice the tomatoes and put them in a colander or large strainer to drain. Turn the bacon over, reduce the heat to medium-low and cook 4 minutes more or until crisp.

03 Meanwhile, trim and quarter the green onions. Put them into a food processor and pulse until coarsely chopped. Crumble or chop the blue cheese and add to the food processor. Add the buttermilk, yogurt, vinegar, Worcestershire, cayenne, black pepper, and salt to taste. (Remember the blue cheese, Worcestershire, and bacon contain a lot of salt.) Puree until smooth. Remove the bacon to a plate lined with paper towels to drain.

04 Cut the turkey or chicken into ½- to ¾-inch cubes. Tap the side of the colander a few times to remove more moisture from the tomatoes, then put the tomatoes in a small bowl. Rinse the colander or strainer used for the tomatoes. Open the can of artichoke hearts into the colander. Gently squeeze out excess moisture from the artichoke hearts. Remove and blot them with paper towels. Cut into quarters.

05 Put the romaine in a large mixing bowl, add 2 tablespoons of the dressing, and toss to coat. Spread out the romaine evenly on a platter or shallow bowl. Place the turkey in a row down the middle of the platter on top of the romaine. Place the tomatoes in two rows on either side of the turkey. Place the artichokes in two rows on either side of the tomatoes. Pour the remaining dressing over the salad across the rows. Chop or crumble the bacon and sprinkle on top.

Greek Bread Salad with Feta Cheese

Italians have their bread and tomato salad, called *panzanella*. In the Middle East, the bread and tomato salad is *fattoush*. The key element in my version of fattoush is mild, perfumed, and sweet Greek or Turkish dried oregano, often sold in bunches in Middle Eastern markets, or by mail (see page 149). Don't use the sharper oregano found on most pizzas. Since oregano is a member of the mint family, fresh mint is a good substitute for the higher-quality oregano.

4 pita breads, preferably whole wheat

8 ounces romaine lettuce or hearts of romaine

1 pound English hothouse cucumbers or Kirby pickling cucumbers

1 to 1½ pounds ripe but firm tomatoes

4 ounces sweet onion such as Vidalia, or mild red onion

¼ cup capers, drained

1 clove garlic

1 lemon

2 tablespoons extra-virgin olive oil

2 tablespoons mild red wine vinegar or balsamic vinegar

1 tablespoon dried Greek oregano or 6 large sprigs fresh mint, enough for ½ cup packed leaves

Salt

Freshly ground pepper

2 ounces feta cheese (preferably sheep's milk), about ¾ cup crumbled

01 Turn on the broiler and adjust the rack about 6 inches from the heat source. Cut the pitas in half by slitting the edges and opening up each pita into 2 thin rounds. Put the 8 halves on a sheet pan. Toast in the broiler just until lightly browned and crisp on one side, about 3 to 5 minutes. (Or toast in a toaster oven.)

02 Meanwhile, trim the top and bottom of the romaine. Cut crosswise into 1-inch-wide strips. Put the strips in a salad spinner and fill with water. Drain and spin dry. Wrap in paper towels to remove excess moisture.

03 While the romaine is drying, trim the ends of the cucumber and cut lengthwise in half, then crosswise into thin half moons. (Scoop out the seeds if using regular cucumbers.) Put into a large mixing bowl. Core and halve the tomatoes and cut into thin wedges. Add to the mixing bowl. Turn the pitas over and toast the other side.

04 Cut off a thin slice from the top and bottom of the onion, halve lengthwise, peel each half, and cut cross-wise into thin half-moon slices. Add the onion to the mixing bowl. Add the capers to the mixing bowl.

05 Remove the pita from the broiler. Peel the garlic. With the motor of a food processor running, drop the garlic down the chute and finely chop. Scrape down the sides of the bowl with a rubber spatula. Juice the lemon. Add the lemon juice, olive oil, and vinegar to the processor. Crush the oregano into the processor with your fingers. Add salt and pepper to taste. Turn on the processor for 15 seconds to mix well.

06 Crumble or cut the feta cheese into small cubes. Tear or crumble the pita bread into the mixing bowl. Add the romaine. Pour the dressing over and toss well. Add the feta, toss again, and serve.

Beef and Beet Salad with Horseradish Cream Dressing

SERVES:	4
CALORIES:	302.43

FAT:	4.41G /13.22%
SATURATED FAT:	1.33G

Beets are the vegetable kids love to hate, but they're a welcome addition to this hearty salad. If you have a bit more time, use fresh beets. I love the crunch and I also like to use the attached greens, which are actually more nutritious than the beets themselves. (Braise them like other bitter greens or put them in soups like Hearty Minestrone, page 106.) This is also a good dish for leftover roast beef, and for cooked potatoes, which are now available in many refrigerated produce cases.

Two large potatoes, preferably Yukon Gold (12 to 14 ounces total)

1 teaspoon salt plus additional for seasoning

1 small head escarole (about 12 ounces)

Canola oil spray

1 pound lean top- or bottom-round steak

Freshly ground pepper

One 15-ounce can diced or sliced beets

6 gherkins (not sweet)

20 chives

2 tablespoons prepared horseradish

½ cup nonfat sour cream or nonfat plain yogurt

2 tablespoons cider vinegar

01   Cut the potatoes into ½-inch cubes. (Do not peel.)
While the hot-water tap runs, put the potatoes and the
1 teaspoon salt in a large saucepan. Barely cover with
hot tap water. Put over high heat and cover. Cook for
10 minutes or until just tender.

02   Meanwhile, fill the sink with cold water while you
remove any damaged leaves from the escarole. Cut the
escarole crosswise into ½-inch-wide strips, discarding the
bottom ½ inch. Add the escarole to the water and wash
quickly and vigorously. Put into a salad spinner and spin
dry. Blot out any excess moisture with paper towels.

03   While the escarole is drying, spray a cast-iron or other
heavy skillet with canola oil spray and put over medium-
high heat. Season the beef with salt and pepper. Add to
the skillet and cook for 2 to 3 minutes on one side.

04   While the beef and potatoes cook, open the can of beets
into a small colander. Rinse briefly then blot dry with
paper towels. If the beets are diced, put them into a
large mixing bowl. If the beets are sliced, stack the slices,
3 or 4 at a time. Quarter each stack. Then add to the
mixing bowl. Cut each gherkin in half lengthwise, then
crosswise into small pieces. Add to the beets. Chop the
chives and add half to the beets. Turn the beef over and
cook for 2 to 3 minutes more, depending on the thickness, for medium-rare.

05   Meanwhile, mix the horseradish, sour cream, vinegar,
and salt and pepper to taste in a small bowl. Put the
escarole in a large mixing bowl. Add 3 tablespoons of
the dressing, and toss to coat. Spread the escarole out
evenly on a large platter.

06   Remove the cooked beef to a cutting board. Cut against
the grain into thin slices about 1-by-½-inch. When the
potatoes are done, drain. Add the beef and potatoes to the
beets. Add the remaining dressing to the beets and beef
mixture and toss well. Place the beef, potato, and beet
mixture on the greens. Sprinkle with the remaining chives.

Taco Salad

SERVES: 4
CALORIES: 318.20

FAT: 10.62g /28.73%
SATURATED FAT: 3.60g

Most taco salads make me cringe: iceberg lettuce, plastic cheese, and deep-fried tortilla shells. Ugh! This one is clean and fresh but still quite satisfying. You might even consider it as part of a warm-weather buffet.

1 pound ripe but firm tomatoes

1 teaspoon salt plus additional for seasoning

1 small head romaine lettuce (about 12 ounces)

6 ounces red cabbage or radicchio

One 15-ounce can red kidney or pinto beans

4 ounces reduced-fat (50 percent) Cheddar cheese

8 ounces sweet onion such as Vidalia

1 tablespoon (or more) sliced pickled jalapeño peppers, drained, or 1 fresh jalapeño pepper

½ cup well-packed fresh cilantro leaves

2 limes

1 tablespoon extra-virgin olive oil

1 tablespoon tequila (may substitute vodka, white wine, or vegetable or chicken stock)

1 tablespoon ground cumin

Freshly ground black pepper

40 baked tortilla chips such as Guiltless Gourmet

01 Core the tomatoes, halve, and cut into thin wedges. Toss with the 1 teaspoon of salt in a colander or large strainer suspended above a small mixing bowl to catch the juices for the dressing. Cut and discard ½ inch from the top and bottom of the romaine. Then cut crosswise into 1-inch-wide strips. Put the strips in a salad spinner. Thinly shred the cabbage with a chef's knife, the large holes of a four-sided grater, or the slicing attachment of a food processor. Add to the salad spinner and fill with water. Drain and spin-dry. Wrap in paper towels to remove excess moisture.

02 While the romaine salad dries, open the can of beans into a colander. Rinse briefly and let drain. Shred the cheese. Cut off a thin slice from the top and bottom of the onion, halve lengthwise, peel each half, and cut crosswise into thin, half-moon slices. Put the onion, romaine, and cabbage in a large mixing bowl. Remove any excess moisture from the beans with paper towels and add to the mixing bowl.

03 With the motor of the food processor running, drop the jalapeño down the chute and finely chop. (If using a fresh jalapeño, stem and seed it first.) Stop the motor and scrape down the sides of the bowl with a rubber spatula. Add ¾ of the cilantro leaves to the processor and pulse a few times.

04 Gently squeeze any excess moisture from the draining tomatoes and reserve the juice. Add the tomatoes to the lettuce mixture. Juice the limes. Put 2 tablespoons of the tomato juice, the lime juice, olive oil, tequila, cumin, and salt and pepper to taste in the food processor with the cilantro and jalapeño. Turn on for 15 seconds to mix well. Add the dressing to the salad and toss well.

05 Put the salad on 4 large plates. Sprinkle the top with the cheese. Lightly crush the tortilla chips over each plate. Chop the remaining cilantro leaves and sprinkle on top.

Vegetarian

Getting more vegetables into our diet is important because nutritionists tell us to cut back on our consumption of red meats and other sources of saturated fat, and because many vegetables have disease-fighting properties. Eating a meatless meal once or twice a week—especially one that doesn't require a lot of time to prepare—is a good way to do that.

But just because you're eating more vegetables and less red meat doesn't mean you can go—you'll pardon the expression—hog wild on oils and other fats. I remember a vegetarian cookbook which had a recipe for grilled tofu with buckwheat noodles and vegetables that called for a cup of oil to marinate the tofu, one-third cup oil to cook the vegetables, and another cup of oil in the dressing. That's about 520 grams of fat just from the oils, which pretty much negates the other healthful aspects of the dish, no matter what kind of oils they are. As with the rest of this book, the recipes in this chapter keep the fat content below twelve grams per serving and under 30 percent of total calories.

If the recipes inspire you to try some fifteen-minute vegetarian dishes on your own, keep in mind a few things. First, you'll need protein substitutes. Canned or frozen beans are the logical first choice, and they are used extensively here and elsewhere in the book. I keep at least three varieties of canned beans—chickpeas, black beans, and cannellini beans—and at least one frozen bean, usually limas, on hand at all times.

Second, go for "meaty" vegetables to sate the appetite. Mushrooms, especially portobellos, are an excellent choice. So is broccoli, which is surprisingly high in protein. A 5.3-ounce serving (about one medium stalk) contains 5 grams of protein.

Third, seek out the freshest produce available, even if it means selecting something you hadn't intended to buy,

much like seafood. Buying what is in season is always preferable, and patronizing local farmers' markets even better, though most of the vegetables used in this chapter and throughout the book are available year round in supermarkets.

You'll notice that a few of the recipes in this chapter seem to be more involved than recipes in other chapters. The major reason is that vegetarian dishes require more chopping of vegetables. You don't have the luxury of just putting a few big pieces of meat in a frying pan.

Nonetheless, all the recipes were cooked by me in fifteen minutes. Your time will depend on your dexterity with a knife or food processor. For example, one of my recipe testers prepared the Burritos with Braised Vegetables and Pumpkin Seeds (page 142) in just over seventeen minutes, while another took thirty-three minutes.

This isn't the only chapter that contains vegetarian recipes. The Pasta chapter has several, including Pasta Primavera (page 91) and Fettuccine with Pesto, Potatoes, and Tomatoes (page 82). In the Salad chapter, there is Greek Bread Salad with Feta Cheese (page 126) and Taco Salad (page 130). Others can easily be converted to vegetarian dishes with a few substitutions. Pasta with Broccoli Raab and Feta Cheese (page 85), Hearty Minestrone (page 106), and Broccoli and Pasta Soup (page 102) all become vegetarian dishes by changing the chicken stock to vegetable stock.

Some dishes in this chapter are already vegan-friendly, like the Spicy Bean and Corn Chili (page 140) and the Couscous Salad (page 137). Others, here and elsewhere (primarily in the Pasta, Salad, and Soups and Stews chapters), can become vegan dishes by cutting out cheese, as in Pasta e Fagioli (page 147).

Vegetable Biryani

SERVES: 4	FAT: 8.93g /16.61%
CALORIES: 451.44	SATURATED FAT: 1.22g

I can't think of another cuisine that makes greater use of spices than Indian cooking. That makes low-fat, if not vegetarian, cooking a lot easier. Wonder if it's possible to make an authentic tasting Indian meal in fifteen minutes? Read what recipe tester Ed Wheeless says: "Having spent some time in Delhi, I've eaten a lot of authentic Indian cooking, and this dish holds its own." If time permits, a raita of yogurt mixed with peeled and grated cucumber would be a soothing accompaniment.

1 cup basmati rice

½ teaspoon saffron threads

1 teaspoon salt plus additional for seasoning

One 10-ounce package frozen baby lima beans

1 tablespoon canola oil

3 cloves garlic

2-inch piece of fresh ginger

1 large onion (about 12 ounces)

1 medium carrot

1 red bell pepper

8 ounces asparagus or green beans

1½ teaspoons curry powder

¼ teaspoon cayenne pepper

¾ cup vegetable stock

⅓ cup packed fresh cilantro leaves

¼ cup dry roasted cashews (about 1 ounce)

½ cup plain low-fat yogurt

⅓ cup raisins

01 While the hot-water tap runs, put the rice in a saucepan. Add 2 cups hot tap water and put over high heat. Add half the saffron threads, crushed between your fingers, and the 1 teaspoon salt. Stir, cover, and bring to a boil. Reduce the heat to low and cook for 10 minutes.

02 Meanwhile, empty the lima beans into a small bowl and add 2 cups hot tap water. Set aside. Put the oil in a 12-inch, nonstick sauté pan over medium heat. Peel the garlic. Peel and halve the ginger. With the motor of a food processor running, drop the garlic and ginger down the chute. While they finely chop, peel the onion and cut into 6 pieces. Add the onion to the food processor and pulse just until chopped. Add the mixture to the sauté pan, raise the heat to medium-high, and stir.

03 Peel and quarter the carrot crosswise. Put in the food processor and pulse just until very coarsely chopped. Add to the pan and stir. Cut the top from the bell pepper. Stand the pepper upright and cut down inside its four walls, separating them from the center core and seeds. Then cut the pepper walls into thin strips with a knife, or coarsely chop in the food processor. Add to the sauté pan.

04 Cut off the bottom inch from the asparagus spears (or the tips of the green beans). Cut the asparagus (or beans) into pieces about 1½ inches long. Add to the pan and stir. Add the curry, cayenne, the remaining saffron, and salt to taste. Stir well. Drain the lima beans and add to the sauté pan with the stock. Stir, cover, and bring to a boil over high heat. Then uncover and cook for about 3 minutes or until almost all the liquid evaporates, stirring a few times.

05 Meanwhile, chop the cilantro leaves. Coarsely chop the cashews. Stir the yogurt and raisins into the sauté pan. Lower the heat to medium or lower to prevent the mixture from boiling.

06 Add the rice to the sauté pan and mix well. Season to taste with salt. Cook for 2 minutes, or until most or all of the liquid evaporates. Stir several times. Pour onto a platter or shallow bowl and top with the cilantro and the cashews.

Couscous Salad

SERVES: 4
CALORIES: 510.96

FAT: 11.83g /20.43%
SATURATED FAT: 1.39g

Couscous, the favorite grain of North Africa, is really a pasta. But this dish isn't your usual pasta salad. As recipe tester Janet Morrissey says, it's "quicker than any pasta salad I've ever made." It's also "crisp and refreshing . . . yet surprisingly filling," says tester Terri Ebaugh. There are several brands of instant couscous on the market. Check the package directions before you proceed with the recipe to make sure the brand you buy requires the same amount of water I use.

½ teaspoon salt plus additional for seasoning

1⅓ cups instant couscous

5 green onions (scallions)

1 small bunch of fresh mint, enough for 1 cup packed
  mint leaves

1 pound Kirby (small pickling) cucumbers or other cucumbers

Two 15-ounce cans chickpeas

1 pound ripe tomatoes

½ cup roasted red bell peppers or pimientos from a jar

⅓ cup drained capers

1 to 1½ lemons

2 tablespoons extra-virgin olive oil

2 teaspoons hot paprika (or 1¾ teaspoons sweet paprika
  and ¼ teaspoon cayenne pepper)

2 teaspoons ground cumin

Freshly ground black pepper

01 Run the hot-water tap. Put 1¾ cups hot tap water in a 2-quart saucepan over high heat. Add the ½ teaspoon salt, cover, and bring to a boil. (Or put the couscous, the ½ teaspoon salt, and 1¾ cups hot tap water in a microwave-safe container. Cover and cook on high power for 6 minutes.)

02 Meanwhile, trim the bulb ends of the scallions, cut in thirds crosswise, and put into a food processor with the mint leaves. Pulse until coarsely chopped. (Or chop by hand.) Put into a large mixing bowl. Trim the ends of the cucumbers but do not peel (unless you are using cucumbers with a waxy skin). Quarter the cucumbers lengthwise, then cut crosswise into ¼-inch-wide pieces. Add to the mixing bowl.

03 When the water in the saucepan comes to a boil, add the couscous, stir, and turn off the heat. Cover and let the couscous steam for 7 minutes. (If using the micro-wave, also let the couscous steam for 7 minutes.)

04 While the couscous steams, open the cans of chickpeas into a colander. Rinse briefly and let drain. Core the tomatoes and squeeze out the juice. Quarter the toma-toes and add to the food processor. Pulse until coarsely chopped. Add to the mixing bowl. Put the peppers in the food processor and pulse until coarsely chopped. (Vegetables may also be chopped by hand.) Add to the mixing bowl along with the capers. Pat any moisture from the chickpeas with paper towels and add to the mixing bowl. Mix the vegetables well but gently.

05 Juice 1 lemon into a small bowl and mix with the olive oil, paprika, cumin, and salt and pepper to taste. Fluff the couscous with a large fork. Add to the mixing bowl with the vegetables. Add the dressing and mix well. Taste and add more salt and the juice from the remaining lemon half if desired.

Spicy Bean and Corn Chili

SERVES:	4	FAT:	3.99g / 7.19%
CALORIES:	459.11	SATURATED FAT:	.21g

If you think chili has to be "con carne" to be satisfying, read what tester Melissa Mersits says about this meatless version: "I have to admit I was skeptical about making this chili, my husband makes a really mean pot of chili, but I was pleasantly surprised. It was quite good." (Mersits and her husband ate two bowls each and had plenty left.) The recipe is spicy but not overpowering. So if you like your chili with multiple alarms, add hot sauce at the table.

1 cup basmati rice

1 teaspoon salt plus additional for seasoning

Olive oil spray

3 cloves garlic

1 tablespoon sliced pickled jalapeño peppers from a jar
   or 1 fresh jalapeño

1 medium onion

1 tablespoon ground cumin

1 tablespoon chili powder

Two 14.5-ounce cans stewed tomatoes

1 cup fat-free vegetable stock

One 15-ounce can black beans

One 15-ounce can kidney beans or pinto beans

2 cups frozen corn

Freshly ground black pepper

½ cup packed fresh cilantro leaves

Hot pepper sauce to pass at the table

01 While the hot-water tap runs, put the rice in a 2-quart saucepan. Add 2 cups hot tap water and the 1 teaspoon salt. Cover and bring to a boil over high heat, then reduce the heat to low and cook for 10 minutes. Turn the heat off and keep covered until ready to serve. (Or put the rice, 2 cups of hot tap water, and the 1 teaspoon salt in a 2-quart, microwave-safe container. Cover and microwave on high power for 10 minutes. Keep covered until ready to serve.)

02 Meanwhile, spray a 12-inch, nonstick sauté pan with olive oil spray and put over medium heat. Peel the garlic. Drop the garlic and jalapeños down the chute of a food processor with the motor running. (If using a fresh jalapeño, stem and seed it first.) When the garlic and jalapeños are finely chopped, stop the motor and scrape down the sides of the bowl.

03 Peel and quarter the onion and add to the food processor. Pulse just until chopped. Add the onion mixture to the pan, increase the heat to medium-high, and stir. Cook for 1 minute. Add the cumin and chili powder and stir well.

04 Open the cans of stewed tomatoes into the food processor bowl (no need to clean the bowl) and pulse just until still slightly chunky. Add the stewed tomatoes and the stock to the pan. Stir well, cover, and bring to a boil.

05 Meanwhile, open the cans of beans into a colander. Rinse briefly and drain. Add the beans and corn to the pan. Stir, cover, and bring to a boil. Uncover and season with salt and pepper to taste. Reduce heat to a simmer and cook for 6 minutes.

06 Meanwhile, chop the cilantro leaves. Stir into the chili just before serving. Serve over the rice. Pass the hot pepper sauce at the table.

Burritos with Braised Vegetables and Pumpkin Seeds

SERVES: 4	FAT: 10.87g /18.81%
CALORIES: 518.08	SATURATED FAT: 1.33g

Think of tortillas like pasta to get an idea of how many ways you can use them. Stuffing tortillas with all manner of vegetables is a good idea for a meatless meal. Vegetables other than those listed below might include broccoli florets, green beans, asparagus, potatoes, carrots, mushrooms, and almost any other leftover cooked vegetable. Because flour tortillas can be quite fattening—and are sometimes made with lard—seek out low-fat tortillas made with vegetable oil and perhaps whole wheat.

Olive oil spray

1 medium to large sweet potato (about 8 ounces)

1 medium red bell pepper

1 medium onion (about 8 ounces)

3 medium zucchini (about 1 pound)

¼ cup dry white wine

1 cup fat-free vegetable stock

Salt

Freshly ground pepper

One 15-ounce can pinto beans or red kidney beans

1 clove garlic

1 tablespoon sliced pickled jalapeño peppers from a jar

½ lemon

½ cup packed fresh cilantro leaves

4 ounces reduced-fat (50 percent) Cheddar cheese

⅓ cup roasted pumpkin seeds

8 low-fat, burrito-size flour tortillas

01 Spray a 12-inch, nonstick sauté pan with olive oil spray and put over medium heat. Peel the sweet potato and quarter lengthwise. Cut crosswise into ½-inch-wide pieces. Increase the heat under the pan to medium-high and add the sweet potatoes.

02 Cut the top from the bell pepper. Stand the pepper upright and cut down inside of its four walls, separating them from the center core and seeds. Then cut the pepper walls into thin strips. Add to the pan and stir. Cut off a thin slice from the top and bottom of the onion, halve lengthwise, peel each half, and cut crosswise into thin, half-moon slices. Add to the pan, increase the heat to high, and stir.

03 Trim the ends from the zucchini and quarter lengthwise. Cut crosswise into ½-inch-wide pieces. Add to the pan, stir, and cook for 1 minute. Add the wine and all but 3 tablespoons of the stock. Season with salt and pepper to taste, cover, and bring to a boil, about 1 minute. Then uncover the pan and allow the liquid to evaporate, stirring once or twice.

04 Meanwhile, in a colander, rinse the beans and let drain. Peel the garlic and drop the garlic and jalapeños down the chute of a food processor with the motor running. When the garlic and jalapeños are finely chopped, stop the motor and scrape down the sides of the bowl. Juice the lemon half. Add to the food processor along with the beans, the remaining 3 tablespoons of stock, and salt to taste. Puree and put into a small bowl.

05 Chop the cilantro leaves and put into another small bowl. Shred the cheese and put into another small bowl. Put the pumpkin seeds into still another small bowl. Spread the tortillas on a microwave safe plate and cover with a paper towel. Microwave on high power for 30 seconds.

06 When the vegetables are tender and no liquid remains in the pan, put them on a platter. To assemble the burritos, smear each tortilla down the center (going left to right) with 1 to 2 tablespoons of bean puree. Add ½ cup of the vegetable mixture over the bean puree, then 1 tablespoon of cheese, 1 teaspoon or more of cilantro, and 2 teaspoons of pumpkin seeds. Fold the bottom up, fold in the sides, and roll into a cylinder. Serve 2 burritos per person.

Creamy Coconut Vegetable Stew

SERVES:	4	FAT:	9.56g /23.83%
CALORIES:	342.48	SATURATED FAT:	4.85g

This colorful stew is not only exotic tasting, it seems downright rich, even when you cut back on the fat by using reduced-fat coconut milk. Vary the vegetables to suit your taste. For example, sweet potatoes, parsnips, or turnips can be used in lieu of potatoes. Cauliflower can replace the broccoli. You can also use green beans, snow peas, or frozen peas.

Canola oil spray

1 pound Yukon gold or red-skinned potatoes

3 cloves garlic

1 medium onion (about 8 ounces)

1 teaspoon ground ginger

1 teaspoon ground coriander

1 teaspoon ground turmeric

½ teaspoon cayenne pepper or to taste

1 cup fat-free vegetable stock

1 bunch broccoli (about 1 pound)

1 red bell pepper

2 small, yellow summer squash or zucchini (8 to 10 ounces total)

One 14-ounce can reduced-fat coconut milk

Salt and freshly ground black pepper

Two pieces (2 to 3 ounces each) packaged Indian naan bread or other flatbread such as pocketless pita

01 Turn on the broiler and put the broiler rack 6 inches from the heat source. Spray a 12-inch, nonstick sauté pan with the oil spray and put over medium heat. Quarter the potatoes lengthwise. (Do not peel.) Then cut crosswise into ½-inch-wide pieces. Add to the sauté pan.

02 Peel the garlic. Peel and quarter the onion. Put both into a food processor and pulse just until chopped. Add the garlic, onion, ginger, coriander, turmeric, and the cayenne to the sauté pan. Increase the heat to high and stir. Cook for 1 minute. Add the vegetable stock, stir, cover, and bring to a boil.

03 Meanwhile, cut the bottom 1 inch from the broccoli stems. Separate the stems from the heads. Peel the stems and cut crosswise into ¼-inch-thick slices. Separate the heads into florets. Add to the pan, stir, and cover. Lower the heat to medium high.

04 Cut the top from the bell pepper. Stand the pepper upright and cut down inside its four walls, separating them from the center core and seeds. Then cut the pepper walls into thin strips. Add to the pan and stir. Trim the ends of the squash, halve lengthwise, then cut crosswise into ½-inch-wide half moons. Add to the pan with the coconut milk and salt and pepper to taste. Stir well, cover, and bring to a boil.

05 Meanwhile, cut the 2 naan or pocketless pitas in half. Spray with the oil spray and put on a sheet pan. Broil 1 to 2 minutes on each side or until browned and lightly crisp. While the bread is toasting, stir the vegetables once or twice and lower the heat to medium. Cook, covered, until the vegetables are tender. Serve in soup plates with the toasted bread.

Pasta e Fagioli

This Italian peasant dish may have humble origins, but like so many dishes of poor immigrants, it's incredibly satisfying. When I was a kid, Mom used to serve it on meatless Fridays topped with ricotta. My version calls for *ricotta salata*, a tangy sheep's milk cheese from Italy (mainly Sicily) that bears little resemblance to the softer, blander ricotta. Feta or a drier-style goat cheese can be substituted.

Olive oil spray

1 medium to large onion (8 to 12 ounces)

4 cloves garlic

One 7-ounce jar roasted red bell peppers

Two 15-ounce cans cannellini beans

½ cup dry white wine

1½ cups fat-free vegetable stock

½ cup packed fresh basil leaves

2 teaspoons salt plus additional for seasoning

12 ounces short fresh pasta such as ziti, rigatoni, or penne, or dried capellini (angel hair)

¼ teaspoon (or more) freshly ground pepper

2 ounces ricotta salata or feta cheese

4 teaspoons extra-virgin olive oil

01   Run the hot-water tap and put 2 quarts hot tap water in each of 2 pots (one large enough to eventually hold all the water and pasta). Cover and bring both pots to a boil over high heat, 8 to 10 minutes.

02   Meanwhile, spray a 12-inch, nonstick sauté pan with olive oil spray and put over medium heat. Peel and quarter the onion. Peel the garlic. Put the onion and garlic into a food processor. Pulse just until chopped. (Or chop by hand.) Add to the sauté pan and stir. Coarsely chop the roasted peppers. Add to the sauté pan, raise the heat to high, and stir.

03   Open the cans of beans into a small colander. Rinse briefly and shake to remove excess water. Add to the sauté pan along with the wine and stock. Cover and bring to a boil, then reduce the heat to a simmer. Meanwhile, stack the basil leaves, roll into a cigar shape, and cut crosswise into thin ribbons. Then chop across the ribbons a few times.

04   As soon as the pasta water boils, transfer the water from the smaller pot into the larger pot and add the 2 teaspoons salt. If using dried capellini, break the pasta in half. Add the pasta to the pot, stir well, cover, and return to a boil. Stir well again, partially cover, and cook for 3 to 4 minutes or until the pasta is done to your taste.

05   While the pasta cooks, add the basil, ¼ teaspoon black pepper, and salt to taste to the beans. Mash half of the beans with a potato masher or the back of a large spoon to thicken the sauce.

06   Crumble, chop, or grate the cheese on the large holes of a four-sided grater. Drain the pasta and add to the bean sauce. Toss well. Add more black pepper if desired. Divide among 4 soup plates. Sprinkle with the cheese and drizzle 1 teaspoon of olive oil over each.

Mail-Order Sources

Coté & Company
800 North Easton Road
Doylestown, PA 18901
215-340-2683
Olive oil, toasted sesame oil, vinegar, cheeses,
instant polenta, pasta, instant couscous, basmati rice

D'Artagnan
280 Wilson Avenue
Newark, NJ 07105
800-327-8246; fax, 973-465-1870
www.dartagnan.com
Venison, duck breasts, game birds and other game,
free-range poultry

Dean & DeLuca
560 Broadway
New York, NY 10012
New York store: 800-999-0306, ext 268, 269, or 282;
fax, 212-334-6183
Catalog: 800-221-7714; fax, 800-781-4050;
www.dean-deluca.com
Olive oil, toasted sesame oil, vinegar, cheeses, prosciutto,
instant polenta, pasta, instant couscous, basmati rice, spices,
kitchen equipment (Note: For more unusual items such as
Asian fish sauce, try the store number.)

Kalustyan's
123 Lexington Avenue
New York, NY 10016
212-685-3451
Spices, fish sauce, toasted sesame oil, basmati rice,
instant polenta, instant couscous

Penzeys Spices
P.O. Box 933
W19362 Apollo Drive
Muskego, WI 53150
800-741-7787; fax, 414-679-7878; www.penzeys.com
Herbs, spices (including gumbo filé powder, chipotle
pepper, and saffron), sesame seeds

Polarica
San Francisco, CA
(800) 426-3872; www.polarica.com
Venison, duck breasts, game birds and other game,
free-range poultry

Smithfield Direct Marketing
One Monette Parkway
Smithfield, VA 23430
800-799-5326
Pork tenderloins, boneless top-loin chops, and center
cut loin roasts (Note: Toll-free number also provides retail
locations in your area.)

Turner New Zealand, Inc.
4675 MacArthur Court Suite 1540
Newport Beach, CA 92660
877-887-6373; www.turnernewzealand.com
Lamb, venison, fish, oysters, squid, shrimp, lobster,
cleaned and cooked mussels and clams

Williams-Sonoma
P.O. Box 7456
San Francisco, CA 94120-7456
800-541-2233; fax, 702-363-2541
www.williams-sonoma.com
Olive oil, vinegar, Parmigiano-Reggiano, nonaerosol oil
sprayers, salad spinners, large skillets and sauté pans, woks,
pasta pots, saucepans, food processors, mandolines, knives,
meat pounders

Index

Table of Equivalents

The exact equivalents in the following tables have been rounded for convenience.

LIQUID/DRY MEASURES

U.S.	Metric
¼ teaspoon	1.25 milliliters
½ teaspoon	2.5 milliliters
1 teaspoon	5 milliliters
1 tablespoon (3 teaspoons)	15 milliliters
1 fluid ounce (2 tablespoons)	30 milliliters
¼ cup	60 milliliters
⅓ cup	80 milliliters
½ cup	120 milliliters
1 cup	240 milliliters
1 pint (2 cups)	480 milliliters
1 quart (4 cups, 32 ounces)	960 milliliters
1 gallon (4 quarts)	3.84 liters
1 ounce (by weight)	28 grams
1 pound	454 grams
2.2 pounds	1 kilogram

LENGTH

U.S.	Metric
⅛ inch	3 millimeters
¼ inch	6 millimeters
½ inch	12 millimeters
1 inch	2.5 centimeters

OVEN TEMPERATURE

Fahrenheit	Celsius	Gas
250	120	½
275	140	1
300	150	2
325	160	3
350	180	4
375	190	5
400	200	6
425	220	7
450	230	8
475	240	9
500	260	10